Unfiltered Truths of Motherhood

Captive & Captivated

SUKA NASRALLAH

Unfiltered Truths of Motherhood: Captive & Captivated

Cover illustration by Suka Nasrallah
Cover art & interior layout by Heidi Sutherlin, www.mycreativepursuits.com

To the three who showed me the
purest form of love, my heartstrings.

And to the one who always
believes in me and encourages me
to soar above and beyond,
the only one who nourishes
the wild sequestered
chambers of my heart,
my better half.

Contents

Introduction

Sometimes in the midst of changing diapers, I feel that part of me has disappeared. I'm missing a piece of the puzzle that is my soul.

> I didn't think I would have to sacrifice this much of myself, just by bringing someone else into this world.

It sounded so simple in my head; how naive I must have been.

I came across my old sketchbook and I thought to myself, who was this person, and where has she gone?

I felt lost.

I didn't recognize who I'd become.

I felt adrift.

I couldn't digest who I was and who I had become.

I felt disorientated.

I didn't realise I had all this emptiness inside of me because I truly felt so full all the time. **Full of love, full of life, full of things to do.**

But all of that was just being busy and consumed by the chronicles of daily life while being a mother. I was giving so much of myself that it didn't even cross my mind that I was actually hollow. I was pouring out of myself without nourishing the void that was leftover. I didn't think motherhood could suffocate me. I didn't think, the root of my happiness—my children—would be the cause of my incapability to get my head floating above the water again.

I felt more dispirited than I have ever felt in my whole life. I felt unenthusiastic. I felt part of my old self dwelling at the surface, trying so hard to be set free, struggling to escape, but remaining trapped.

I felt imprisoned by motherhood.
I did not recognize myself nor these
feelings I was having because I had
suppressed them for so long.

I didn't know I could miss a time when my life was emptier than it was now.

My heart is so full, but why do I feel lacking?

I'm too deep in the waters, too invested in the family I've built. Which is beautiful and rewarding in many ways, but it came at an extortionate cost. The cost of my dreams. As I sit here, I ponder on who I was and who I could have been had the circumstances been different. But I assure myself this is the farthest it can go, pondering and contemplating.

For now, I'm self-preserving.
I'm accepting my reality.
Patience, I tell myself.
It will pass, I tell myself.
All in good time, I tell myself.

And here I am today, making one of my biggest dreams come true. Writing my very own book. Sometimes we treat our dreams as if they were unattainable and that is a mistake. We must dream and hope in order to keep ourselves motivated in aspiring to do greater. My time has come, and it was worth the wait.

My children were worth the sacrifice. They inspired me. Through them, I found the courage to voice my words and to put my pen to my paper. I'm grateful for the feelings of emptiness because within them I met a version of myself I never thought existed.

Motherhood, in all its fragility, encompasses the darkest you will endure while also shining a light on you so intense that you feel it in the depths of your soul. Just as you are bringing a child into this world, you as well are going through a birthing process.

Embrace your journey.

Chapter 1
Be Still My Heart

I am a shambling vessel
for everyone's wants and needs.
Every want and every need lingers
on my person. I am mama.

Motherhood will weaken your heart. The same heart you feel can withhold any pain to protect your young, that same heart will now shatter over a scraped knee. Motherhood will turn your nerves from peaceful and composed to unsteady and fragile. It is by far the most beautiful and mesmerising journey I have been on, but in all honesty, it has sucked the life right out of me.

I'm not only talking about the physical toll it will take on you, the sleepless nights that make your eyes burn and your heart weary, the pounding headaches from the constant screaming, the back pain from carrying your little throughout the day and night, the sore shoulders from hunching down while breastfeeding. I'm not talking about all the physical pain your body endures, though it is very relevant.

I'm talking about a love so immensely and deeply embedded in the mortar of who you are, and also a love that can rip your heart to shreds; a crippling love. A love that sometimes leaves me quivering with no sense of control over myself, yet simultaneously has quite literally engulfed my whole existence. It has defined me. It brought me to realise that being a mother wasn't made for the weak-hearted like me, but I could swear that becoming a mother is exactly what made me this way.

Was this just part of the package? You know, having to give up so much of yourself to become who your family and children need you to be—having to transform and delegate. Because that's what moms have to do. They must be present in any way a situation calls for them.

Where I once stood filled with confidence and courage, I found myself standing still and fearful and full of questions and doubts.

Unsure about what was right and what was wrong. That's kind of expected to happen to you though when the decisions you're making are about another person's well-being and survival. It's not just black and white anymore.

I found myself fearful because I had so much love to give to my littles, and all I wanted was for them to feel and know love. I wanted them to know it like it was their primary language. I wanted them to speak its language and sway within its realm. But I was so scared because this world I'm setting them off into is so cold and shrill, and how was I to know how much love was too much love to give? How much love would make them weak and incapable of fending for themselves?

Being a mother made me weak to a point where I would cry whenever my child felt left out with friends. My empathy plays a role but motherhood, motherhood in itself is what makes your heart's enclosure delicate and flimsy. I would sit next to his bed at night and caress his soft cheek ever so gently, praying that I can take his pain away.

Praying that my hugs and kisses will suffice for a little longer.

Praying I will be his safe haven for as long as we both live.

But in reality, knowing that at one point or another, I just won't be able to protect his little heart from breaking.

I am not prepared for the day when I will have

no control. I am not prepared to live a life where I have no ability to heal their fragile hearts with a kiss on the cheek and a warm embrace.

I know a day will come where I will not be capable of making them feel better simply by holding their heads against my beating heart, and that brings me so much pain. I know one day I will have no control and I am not prepared for that.

How can I ever be when they are my reason?

Who will protect them?

How can anyone ever do my job?

My job of loving them so deeply and protecting them with all my might. I worry about a future in which their mother won't be guiding them along the way. I worry so much in my journey with them. I worry about things completely out of my hands and that is why motherhood broke me. It broke me in ways I feel I can never be mended.

Motherhood has put me in a state of constant grief—always grieving a stage that has passed, that I didn't enjoy as much as I should have. My heart is always aching at the thought of losing them eventually, not having them within arm's reach. I have become so wary of this callous world and its rigid edges.

Motherhood doesn't last forever.

And with all its glory and beauty, motherhood gave me a heart that shatters over a scraped knee.

Motherhood has made me weak.

Chapter 2

Perfect Mothers Don't Exist

Being whole is not defined
by perfection, for perfection
in itself is merely a perception.

It's your choice, and it's how you choose to see things. It's all dictated by what lens you're looking through. Are you being optimistic or pessimistic? You can blossom on your own terms without the need of an audience or a stage; validation from others isn't what you need.

Motherhood in itself is a journey tailored to each and every mother and her own ways, based on her own choices. Not only is it possible, but very normal to be imperfectly perfect. That is what motherhood is in itself. It's so not normal yet so normal. It's indifferent. It's so unique to every person and that's the beauty in it.

We're all on this journey together as a whole, but

we're all living out different stories. Some people endure pain and to them, it's about embracing the journey and growing with and through the pain. Through their individual path. Some people learn to endure and cannot unlearn those ways and that becomes who they are—they will find themselves defined by that.

While most mothers do truly believe that the perfect mom is a stereotype, most of us still feel the pressure to be perfect; to do all the right things the right way based on what people around us are saying. You must learn to trust yourself on this journey and you must truly believe deep in your heart that you were made for this. You were put on this path for a purpose and that purpose lies within you; only you can uncover it. Body image, parenting styles, food choices, there are so many opinions. But that's all they are—opinions. You were made for your children as they were made for you.

You hold the power here.

It's hard to step away from all the surrounding subliminal messages, but you must realise that everything you see around you is just a snippet of someone's life, a snippet that they're choosing to share. Sure, we all want that perfect picture with the perfect little grin that highlights our babies' dimples.

We always want to show and prove that we're doing our very best. We all want to be validated. But how much of that is real life? How long will we keep pushing ourselves to the point of breaking only to be deemed good enough?

> **The reality of it is most of my days include me dragging myself to keep up with my house and every chore that it entails in order to keep my family afloat.**

The messy moments that encapsulate my days are in reality the best moments. The moments that happen naturally, that aren't staged, the moments I rarely share. They are the moments I will remember and cherish. The sticky handprints smeared on my patio doors and window. The ketchup-covered table after my children have their favorite meal; if you ask me, that's everything a perfect day entails. That's when I feel the most accomplished.

Real moms don't look perfect when they leave the house. I'm always a mess at school drop- offs because my mornings are hectic and busy. Because I don't have time to focus on painting a fresh face of makeup when I'm rushing to make three lunches and three breakfasts and to repeat simple instructions100 times—yes, the same instructions I've been saying every single morning for as long as I can remember. Nor am I a perfect mother when I'm hurrying my children out the door, begging them to put their shoes on and to stop fighting.

What I am is a real mom.

I'm busting my butt to give my children the best life I can give them, a life filled with unconditional love and support. And that is what I call imperfectly perfect. Me giving it my all, all the time. Even when I have nothing left to give. I'm giving it everything I've got and then some.

Everyone thinks they're going
to be the perfect mother
until they become one.

Those that judge and say they'll never give their kids fast food and screen time are the mothers that will find themselves at the McDonald's drive-thru one day more than they'd like every week.

Be cautious not to immerse yourself in the social media life that only shows you the best parts, rather submerse yourselves in real motherhood and all the joy it entails because in its messiest moments, you are giving and receiving so much love.

Perfect mothers do not exist.
Good enough mothers make mistakes,
that's inevitable and that's ok
and that's necessary.

That is the only way we can improve. No one ever learned from a perfectly clean slate. Enjoy the ride as rocky as it may be because trust me, it's worth it.

Chapter 3
Childbirth Forever Adjusted Me

Childbirth is a journey that runs through you as deep as the forest, going farther than the naked eye can see and deeper than ears can hear. It's a journey more intense and sacred than you can comprehend, and you were chosen to experience and endure it.

A journey that takes you wholeheartedly into a world inexplicably filled with bewilderment and fascination—pure bliss and intoxication, exhilarating and liberating to witness such power within yourself—right at the end of your fingertips, within your reach, radiating from you.

Raw and real.

This is the most human I've ever felt.

Through the phases, I have evolved. From the minute the seed was planted inside my womb, to the moment I brought life to my side of the world and held it in my arms. I felt such a surge of responsibility overcome me.

Such a treasure to cherish.

Such a blessing.

And at that moment, I was forever adjusted. I felt as if my whole purpose was rekindled and from that moment on, I've been passing through rebirth after rebirth, in every phase I've been through with my children on this journey. Every passing day, every milestone seems like a brand-new voyage.

Sometimes, I worry I will no longer remember their young days, their babbling days, their crawling days. I worry it may be just a glitch in my mind eventually and not a clear, vivid image. I worry all their early incarnations will slip through my mind much too quickly.

Is it just a constant state of nostalgia I will be in until the end of time? Will I continue to look forward with one foot constantly rooted in the past, struggling to let go?

How quickly I forgot the pain of bringing you into this world and how quickly I began thinking of our goodbyes. Motherhood has a way of doing that, ripping you apart at the seams almost quite literally, but binding you together with the simplest glistening in your babies' eyes.

Childbirth had me flooded with joy and fear. And since that moment, I've known nothing but the deepest love there has ever been. I have never felt more intense emotions than I did when my child was first put on my chest, raw, covered in vernix, crying, and fluttering like a bird.

The fragility of the relationship between a mother and her young is like a delicate spool of thread. She wraps her existence to completely surround this human whom she has created from the depths of her soul. She is a creation that is devoted wholeheartedly to the wellbeing of another. Hers is an eternal sacrifice. She endures suffering while relentlessly braving the road. Filled with determination even though she feels she is lacking. Her purpose is fueled by the security of her young.

Rummaging past her insecurities which are many, her feelings of incompetence which never seem to fade, in hopes of burying them deeper in order to withstand the storms and sustain her promise.

A mother is a force unaltered and unmatched. Ask for a superhero and I'll show you a mother.

A mother has no visible finish line.

Motherhood is born through you and goes with you to the grave. It is learned through the gift of time, one cry at a time, one sleepless night at a time, one teething baby at a time, one sick child at a time, one bullied child at a time, one lonely child at a time, one healthy and happy child at a time.

Motherhood is learned but cannot be taught. They can speak for days in your ears with advice that will seem to stand, but no one can teach you how to mother the children you have been given, no one, except motherhood itself.

This is your life's work that will come to define your existence. Every moment serves a purpose, so I urge you to embrace every occurrence. Every moment is inexplicably significant and unlike any other.

Chapter 4

Hormones and Flesh Over Ice

Everyone's fawning over this
perfect baby while I'm just here,
simply existing. I'm torn apart at my
most delicate parts, sewn back together
like a piece of tulle, barely holding.

Swollen.

Exposed.

Raw.

Empty.

Confused.

In shock.

Overwhelmed.

I'm a cocktail of hormones and flesh over ice.

Everyone's cradling my new baby while I'm

leaning against a wall, praying my legs will hold me up just a little while longer so I don't collapse and humiliate myself. *Please God*, I plead, *save me the embarrassment of not looking absolutely well kept.*

Everyone's in awe with every breath my new baby takes, taking in every smirk, every grimace, every little sound, every cry, every wince, while I can barely keep my eyes dry long enough to get a good look.

You see, I haven't been able to fully grasp the extent to which my life has changed completely overnight, maybe this is why I'm struggling to understand how everyone else can be so completely euphoric. These early stages of motherhood, these days that have birthed me into a new person and given me this new responsibility, they have also put me in a rut.

I'm torn between loving every inch of this perfect creation while simultaneously having heavy, heavy feelings. Towards myself, towards my new baby, towards this new life I've been born into all at once.

Feeling lost.

Feeling bare.

Feeling vacant.

Feeling inept.

I find myself wishing you were still inside of me keeping me safe while I keep you safe. I fear for you now. I worry about you now. Feeling unprepared because one cannot faultlessly and genuinely tell you how it's going to be. No one can prepare you for the volcano of emotions ready to erupt inside you. After all, how can someone prepare you for having terrifying, fleeing feelings like these?

Feelings, I'm told will pass.
Dangerous feelings, I fear, will not pass.

I'm shown love and support that only goes as far as the baby's health. The support is limited to my physical state.

If my body heals, I look well and kept,
and I'm expected to have it all together.

While my parts have taken the thread and embraced it, my heart was shattering and bursting at the ridges. My body embraced the care and thrived, but it's my heart that I worry about.

There is no thread that can mend an aching heart and a weary soul.

And while I'm also fawning over my new baby, I'm battling emotions far greater than I knew existed. I'm battling them silently because that seemed more acceptable than

getting help.

Because people will tell me, "You're just tired and need some sleep," and "This will pass." Because it's not talked about enough.

Because new mothers are just handed some pamphlets and sent off into the world with a delicate being that they are now solely and completely responsible for keeping alive. Being told, "It will come to you, you're a natural, you've got this mama." While I admire the encouragement, that is not what will hold me up during the long nights to come.

Meanwhile, you haven't even begun to comprehend what being called 'mama' means. The toll that word will take on you. The weight of bearing it. It is a whole new world on its own. A world you have just been sent into, arms flailing, eyes watering, heart racing, fear creeping.

The early days of motherhood
are dangerous and intimate.
You're treading towards rough waters
and barely catching a breath.

Frightful of slipping an inch lower so you don't

submerge yourself completely under the tremendous weight of this body of water encompassing you, fearful of drowning in this new world of bittersweet love.

It is much harder than it looks and believe me when I tell you it will take a village. A village of present people, willing people, devoted people. A village that will be there during the long nights when your eyes are burning and your arms are numb. When you find yourself asleep on the rocking chair with your baby nestled on your chest, slipping slowly until by the grace of God you're woken up to tighten your grip. Yes, it happens. Exhaustion gets the better of you and your eyes will just give out sometimes.

A village of people that will be there to carry the weight with you. The weight of not recognising yourself in your new body and learning to love and embrace the stripes that have drawn valleys on your skin.

A village of people that will tell you to give yourself some grace.

A village of people who will understand that a colicky baby just needs to be held all the time and who hold him with you when you are no longer capable.

A village that will hold you while you sob hopelessly with not a clue in the world of what you should be doing next.

A village that will carry you for as long as you may

need to be carried—minutes, hours, days, months, or years.

Mothers need to be cared for
just as much as their newborns.

They are the utmost fundamental part of the equation and they cannot be overlooked and dismissed so easily.

Mothers are just as fragile as the babies they bring into this world. They need love and care and attention.

They are helpless in these early stages, just as their newborns.

They are emotions and flesh over ice.

Chapter 5

Postpartum Depression: You're Not Broken

Postpartum is simply the phase that follows childbirth. Postpartum Depression is depression suffered by a mother following childbirth, typically arising from the combination of hormonal changes, psychological adjustment to motherhood, and extreme fatigue. But I refer to that whole period of time as a drunken haze in which you're simply drifting, coexisting, unknowing if you're living; if you're tangible.

If someone touched you, would you feel it?

You're not quite sure.

You feel incapable of grasping the reality that is your life now.

It came as a sudden shock and you haven't been able to move past that stage. A new world dumped on you overnight with a weight heavier than you can hold. Yet here you are. No sign of a way out. You're blooming like a delicate flower, being the most beautiful you ever were, only to lose parts of yourself just as the rose petals fall and wither away. You become one with purpose, only here for the bigger picture. Just riding the waves, going up and down however they may take you. You are on a ride with no set destination in sight, forgetting the details of what your life once was.

You're wearing a disguise that's become who you are.

You're fighting a battle no one knows about and keeping up with this image that you're trying to portray—the forced smile—the image of being 'okay'.

You're dreading to face any inconvenience, no matter how minor. You're afraid to have to face your feelings.

You're afraid of being made.

Your broken heart is aching, and you don't really understand what is happening.

Why are you feeling all of this pain as though it has become one with you?

It has become who you are.

It now defines you.

Intertwined together like the roots of a tree embracing the earth beneath it.

It has you feeling helpless and exposed.

Worrying that at a moment's notice you could just break. I know you feel trapped but I'm here to tell you there is an outlet. The instant reaction is to give up, because it's so, so heavy, this burden you're carrying. But hang on just a little longer. Look deep into your soul and find that strength and resilience you know you have. Know that through your pain, you made it this far, and know that there is so much you still haven't seen.

This little baby wants to grow with you.

This little baby loves you no matter what, no matter how.

Those around you who want nothing except to see you well and happy, turn to them. Hang on to them as you navigate your way along this rocky road.

Know that it doesn't end here.
You won't always be this way.

You won't always be this way, because there are people and things in place to help you. You just need to be willing. You need to truly understand that you are worthy and needed and wanted and loved and strong enough to persevere.

Just as the leaves are reborn with every season,

welcome your new season by detaching your old leaves. Nourish your soul and stand in the sunlight. Seek the helping hand. We are gifted with ***time***, and ***although time does not heal all wounds, it softens the edges of trauma.***

The light will find its way in, even if through the smallest crack, the light will always find its way in. And those broken vessels will be filled with a shining light that will always make way for healing.

Embrace the light.

You are not broken.

You are human.

You are feeling.

Seek the help. Know that you are worth it. Know that postpartum depression doesn't happen because of you, it happens to you, and through it, you learn, and you grow. Accept the help.

Accept the medications. Accept the support. Seek it out and let it in.

There is no shame in getting help.

Chapter 6

When the Form of My Baby Became That of a Toddler

If you're lucky enough, you'll notice the little details changing; the things you usually don't pay attention to because you've become so accustomed to them in your everyday life. The mundane specifics that you tend to look past because they're so easily accessible since they are right there in your face, sunrise to sundown. But if you're lucky enough, you'll notice their eyes widen. What once were small little circles, are becoming almond-shaped eyes that glisten and speak to your soul.

You'll notice the form of a baby becoming that of a toddler. If you're lucky enough, you'll notice their fingers get longer and less stubby. The little dimples on their hands will be no longer. You'll notice their voices become more clear and less raspy. For now, they still have some softness to their words, but before you know it, they will sound so grown up and pronounce their s's perfectly.

If you're lucky enough, you'll notice today may be the last day they fit into these little shoes, and you'll sit there with them, tears filling your eyes, wondering just where the time has gone.

> **You'll notice this whole journey is a series of lasts. Our days are not guaranteed, and every moment is not at all like its predecessor. When a moment presents itself, and you can't tell whether it might be the last time, you will allow it to encompass your whole being. You will get lost in that moment.**

Do we ever really get to bear witness to all these lasts?

Or do they pass us by so swiftly leaving us with mere memories that will soon enough be challenging to recall?

Do you ever truly enjoy the last time you rock your baby to sleep? How could you? How could you know this would be the last time? Until the years have passed and you're cleaning out your storage room and you get a glimpse of that rocking chair and you wonder. You will try so hard to remember the last time. And it will fill your heart with a paradox of both joy and melancholy. Pondering what once was and what is now. Bittersweet.

> *Do you ever wonder if today will be the last time you tend to a scraped knee?*

> *Do you wonder when you will be humming that*

lullaby for the last time?

Do you ever think about how nostalgic parenthood is?

It takes you on this roller coaster of emotions that you don't really ever get off and those feelings stay with you. The excitement of watching them grow is also a cloud of gloom surrounding your days. You'll notice that ***our life is a series of lasts*** and you'll notice that there's not much we can do about it except soak in every moment. Breathe it in like it's the oxygen we depend on for survival.

Sometimes, it's ok if you leave the laundry to pile up if it means making room for those special moments.

The mess is not going anywhere but your children are growing at a startling rate, and you're already missing so much every time you blink.

Chapter 7
My Life Without You

It's hard to imagine that one day you're not going to want to be carried by me.

What purpose would my arms have
if not to hold you?

It's hard to imagine that one day, you won't want to snuggle. You won't want to be kissed countless times. You won't seek sanctuary in me.

It's hard to accept that one day when you're taller than me and I hold you close, my arms may not fit comfortably around you.

It's hard for me to accept that soon enough you will have a life of your own, a life in which you may not want me to be fully involved.

What will I do with myself

when that day comes?

It's very hard for me to accept that you will no longer need me on a daily basis when I am here for you.

You won't need me to tie your shoes, nor match your clothes, nor comb your hair, nor pack your lunch.

It's hard for me to accept the reality that is life; that we're in a race where no one wants to make it to the finish line. A race that no one wants to win.

It's hard for me to accept that you will not always be with me, you will not always be part of my day. You won't be the face I see in the morning nor the face I see before bed.

I will not always be the one waking you up, I will not always be the one seeing you off at the door. It's only a matter of time before someone comes to take my place.

It's so very hard for me to accept that while I'm in the trenches with you now, I will not be your focal point for much longer.

It's so very hard for me to accept that one day you will outgrow me the way you outgrew your newborn onesies in what felt like a blink of an eye. I desperately wanted you to grow up so fast so I may see the wonderful things you would accomplish, but I wasn't careful what I wished for, and now all I want is for time to go backward.

It's so very hard for me to imagine a life where I don't wake up an hour before you to prepare your lunch, where I don't schedule my appointments around you.

It's hard for me to imagine just what my life will be like without you.

Who will I be?
What will become of me?

The day you were born I wasn't myself anymore. I didn't live for myself. I was reborn for you, to revolve around you. You are the sun, and I am a planet orbiting you, needing you so desperately.

And now that I sit and think that one day, I may have that quiet life again, I can't imagine what I would do with it. I don't want that anymore. As much as I struggled in those early years, all I want is for them to come back, and for time to stand still. All I want is to be a mama of littles again. All I want is to be your everything, for just a little while longer.

I can't imagine wanting to be anything else, anything other than mama. I can't imagine finding fulfillment in anything other than your presence and your voices around me. Filling the walls of our home with laughter and joy. I simply cannot fathom this truth. I can't, rather I don't want to.

What kind of life will I have if it's not revolving around you?

Where can I tap out?

Where can I press pause?

I sit here and I think about scenario after scenario, and I come up empty-handed. In no way does this end like a fairy tale. In no scenario, no "normal" scenario, will you remain mine until the end of time.

In no scenario does this
end without tears; happy or sad.
Without heavy hearts
being forced to bid farewell.

I find myself longing for your giggles, years after your voice has gotten too deep.

I find myself yearning for the sight of your shoes piled up near the entryway. And at the end of it all, I'm sitting in an empty house, with only the echoes of your voices dwelling in its walls, with only memories of your shadows as you leaned on the kitchen counters. At the end of it all, I'm left with memories.

At the end of this chaos, when you've decided it's time for you to grow on your own, I have

one last wish for you. I pray with my whole heart and all my being, I pray with every bone in my body, that you truly know I am here.

As long as my heart is beating, it's beating for you.

As long as I'm breathing, every last breath is for you.

As long as I'm on this earth, my whole existence is for you.

My love for you will stretch as long as the miles that may come between us, though if it were up to me, I would have the biggest house possible to keep you and whomever you may want to add, under my wing.

My love for you will fill the lonely gaps between the phone calls. My love for you will forever shine on my gloomy days without you.

When you become big, my little one, my love will never fade.

Chapter 8
You Taught Me Everything I Know

Forgive me my son, my first love.

My lessons learned.

My oops and uh-ohs.

My love story and my life lessons.

Forgive me.

My eldest.

My young man, the one who made me a mother.

You named me mama.

And what an honor it was.

I remember waiting so impatiently to hear your first word, praying so hard it would be 'mama' as if that was the standard in which they measured good mothers by and I wanted so desperately to be the best mother I can be for you.

Where do I begin with you? How do I begin to express my feelings for you and how I can make you truly understand your worth? You're so precious to me I'm not sure I have the right words without sounding obsessive.

Forgive me.

I know I put so much responsibility on you without you even understanding; without me even realising what I was doing. I was learning about a whole new world through you, and I expected you to carry some of the burden with me.

I didn't know any better, forgive me.

You were my trial and error in everything that I know today.

You were my first for everything.

You were my first baby bath,

First nail clippings,

First diaper change,

First fever, your firsts were mine as well.

And I was so scared. I was afraid of messing it all up and I was relying on you to guide me.

Forgive me.

My goodness if I could go back, I would like to believe that I'd try to be more prepared so I wouldn't have to learn through you but who am I kidding? What could possibly prepare anyone to have their heart beating outside of their body?

You taught me to slow down during our short days and long nights together. Things got dark for me, but you were always there lighting the way.

You taught me I was capable of caring for you through the fevers and the meltdowns.

You taught me that it didn't matter what kind of stroller I bought you and what brand your onesies were, they all clothed you just the same.

You taught me what was really important and what deserved my attention.

You taught me to look at life through a different lens and I'm so grateful I did.

You have anchored me when I didn't even know I needed to be grounded.

Forgive me, because I realised that all along you were teaching me about the world when I'm the one who was supposed to be doing the teaching. Forgive me for putting all of that pressure on you.

Becoming your mother had me in shambles but you held my hand every step of the way; you guided me along the right path.

You are my prized possession.
You are all my wins.

Forgive me for all the times I wanted to give

up, it was never about you, it was about my fear of inability.

But that glimmer of hope in your eyes that would meet mine every time you'd look at me always pushed me farther. Pushed me to do better. Never underestimate the power of love.

If you're lucky enough, it gets you through. And your love got me through my sweet firstborn.

You taught me how to give love so intensely, so selflessly, it actually, physically hurts.

You taught me this is what it is to be a mother.

You taught me sacrifice.

You taught me patience.

You taught me dedication.

You taught me discipline.

Forgive me for needing all these life lessons from you.

All this you did for me and so much more. So, I truly ask for your forgiveness because I feel that I've put the weight of the world on your shoulders. I simply couldn't do it without you. Loving you is the only thing that got me through. Forgive me my firstborn, the one who made me mama. Forgive me for needing you to encompass me in order for me to survive.

Chapter 9

I Am the Mother of a Strong-Willed Child

My firstborn was so unique in all ways. He was a dream come true for me and everything I ever wished for as a first-time parent.

I prayed for him from the bottom of my heart.

I prayed for this little boy.

I imagined his voice.

I imagined his first cry.

I imagined the curls that would sit on top of his head.

I imagined his 10 fingers and 10 little toes.

I imagined everything there was to imagine and I dreamt of the day he would rest in my arms.

Until he did and my dreams came true. He was the most perfect little boy I had ever met. And as the days passed by, as he grew older, I became aware that my little boy was as strong-willed as they came. He was here challenging me in every way possible; more ways than I could have imagined, for sure.

Early on, it felt like too much to handle. Being a first-time mom and not having the easiest newborn had its trials.

I knew this boy was special.

I knew he would teach me so much.

I just wasn't sure if I was capable of being everything he needed.

I wasn't sure just how far this trait would grow with my son.

Was it just a phase of being a difficult newborn? Was it something that would pass as he hit his first year milestone? I truly didn't know and could not see the light at the end of the tunnel. I was taking it one day at a time and learning and growing alongside my strong-willed child.

I learned that having a strong-willed child meant that I would not get more than two hours of uninterrupted sleep for the first year of his life, and it meant learning to function that way.

It meant that I let him cry at night in hopes of sleep training him.

It meant learning to do all my housework by holding him in the baby carrier because he was only happy in my arms, swaying to my unique rhythm.

It meant adjusting my back to hold his arms up and guide him when he insisted on learning to walk at eight months old until he mastered it.

It meant knowing that he would just try another way when I said 'no' because,to him, it meant a challenge.

It meant accepting that things will happen at his own pace. I constantly found myself saying, "When the time is right."

It meant he may not take the path I wanted him to, but the one he chose was more pleasing to the eyes, so I'll marvel at his love for beauty.

It meant he wanted to perfect any task he began, and there was no way he would give up, no matter no how.

And if it didn't pan out how he desired, I had to absorb his frustration and welcome the meltdown with open arms, because this was him. He was determined in his ways because that was all that made sense to him. It meant I had to think outside of the box in order to engage and captivate his remarkableness.

Because he is nothing shy of that.

Remarkable.

It meant being head-to-head with a professional negotiator because he was good!

It meant accepting that I now lived with a kid who was more powerful than me and who always had to say the last words. Who came out on top relied solely on me giving into his relentlessness. And when I didn't, boy we don't want to go down that road because it got very loud, very fast. And everyone ended up in tears.

My strong-willed boy did scare me at the beginning of our journey together. He tested me so much, but he also taught me so much.

My strong-willed boy broke me
more times than I can count,
but he also saved me.

He reminds me every day that God chose me to be his mama and that we were made for each other. Each new day I learn patience and grace. I have learned to brave the storm for him, through him, and with him. And it has taught me the most valuable lessons. He taught me that he is so determined but will always need me. We embrace the commotion that is our life because it is lovely in its own way.

I have learned that there's nothing wrong with being strong-willed. The schools will try to label it. People around us often say, "Maybe you should get him checked out." People always want to have some input in the situation, but no one seems to accept him for who he is.

He is impeccable.

He is nothing less than a perfect little boy, no matter what people tell me. I will embrace his liveliness and I will continue to be proud of him.

I will forever remember the adventures he put me through.

Chapter 10

I'm Sorry Mama

I'm sorry mama for the trouble I always cause.

I'm sorry that I'm too much for you sometimes.

I'm sorry that I make you look forward to bedtime and nap time.

I'm sorry that sometimes you cry at night after my siblings and I go to bed.

I know how tired you are all the time because you're always telling me, "I'm tired- please keep it down".

I'm sorry that I just don't know how to use indoor voices. It's much more fun to be loud and I love having fun.

I'm sorry that I always have so much to say. I know I ask you a thousand questions a day, but you just know everything about everything, and I want to be as smart as you.

I'm sorry you're always worrying about me getting hurt or hurting someone. I don't like trouble; I just love jumping around everywhere.

I'm a curious little boy, don't you know?

I'm sorry I'm always bickering with my siblings, but I was here first, and they should know you were my mommy first; they should know I'm the leader. I want all your attention on me, mama. I just miss you, mama.

I'm sorry for all the things I do but there's just something in me that's always telling me to do the opposite of what you say and it's kind of funny to me. I like to do things my own way because I know I'm smart. I know it will impress you in the end. I just want to find my own way. Why do I have to follow yours?

I'm sorry that you feel like I'm challenging, I hear you complaining to dad that I drove you crazy. But you challenge me, too. Can't we just be friends? Can't we just support each other?

I'm sorry that I'm so difficult mama. But I know I'm capable of greatness, only if you'd let me be.

I feel like I can conquer the world,
just if you'd let me be.
I just need some space.
But you're always trying to contain
me and I want so badly to be free.

You're always worrying about me, and I know I scare you, but trust me I'm brave enough. You've taught me so well, mama.

I'm not sure why I was made this way, but I know God made us all special in our own way; that's what you always tell me after all. Maybe I'm just a little extra special.

Please mama, when I'm giving you a hard time and I yell and scream for you to leave me alone, and I push you away, please, don't leave me just yet. Don't give up on me. I know I need you; I just always feel like I have something to prove.

Promise me, mama, no matter how far I push away, you'll always be there to guide me back. I'm just a kid who needs some more time.

I'm just a curious kid.
I'm just a daring kid.
I'm just an excited kid.
But I'm just a kid.
A kid that will always need his mama.

So, please mama, don't let me go just yet.

Chapter 11

I Don't Want to Miss a Thing

A picture is worth a thousand words like they say, so most days, I'm the mom holding her phone and snapping pictures of my kids left and right, not wanting to miss a single moment. I am taking it all in through the lens of my camera.

I'm the mom always telling my kids to, "say cheese" and getting frustrated when they don't cooperate.

Why do I do it?

Why the headache?

Why don't I just live in the moment?

Well because, plain and simple, the moment won't suffice for me.

I want to sit after a long day of playing and fighting and tantrums and tears and laughs and giggles and be able to look back and watch every moment again because I worry a day will come when all I'll have are the memories, and that won't be enough for me.

I want to be able to see the scratch on my son's cheek in a picture and remember when and how it happened; remember the tears and remember the countless hugs and kisses.

I want to remember the color of the shorts he was wearing that day.

I want to remember which bow was holding back my daughter's hair.

I want to remember what dress she wore and the fact that she now has an opinion of what she wears.

I want to remember my son's shoes that were once white but are now stained with dirt, proof of the adventures he's been on, proof of the memories he's made, proof of the fun he's had. I want it all and I don't want to risk not remembering.

There will come a day when I will find myself telling someone, "those were the good old days" and I want to be able to look back at them and remember.

I want to be able to feel everything I was feeling while taking the picture—the immense love. I want to capture it all while I can.

I want their glistening eyes to stay with me forever, even if in the future only through a camera lens. And so, I will forever be "that" mom.

Chapter 12
Boy Mama

You see, I have these two boys and I have the weight of the world on my shoulders.

I'm Lebanese, and in my culture, having a boy is seen as a triumph, a victory. While having a girl is a burden, a responsibility very heavy to hold because you want to raise her to be the perfect wife and mother one day. Having a girl comes with immense pressure.

If you ask me, that's all backwards.

To raise a boy is not the simplest task. I find it much heavier an assignment than raising a girl, only if we must compare, though I despise comparisons. To raise a boy is to raise a man.

A man,
A husband,
A father,
A brother,
An uncle,
A friend.

To raise a boy is to sculpt a man, where a double

dose of kindness and respect is much needed.

To raise a boy is to give love.

So. Much. Love.

Pure, endless, limitless love.

To raise a boy is to shower him with encouragement and douse him with affection. To raise a boy is to show him that it's ok to cry. It's ok to feel. To raise a boy is to show him that he cannot hold double standards.

You see, to raise a boy, you can't only think of his future. You need to think of his partner, his children. You need to take into consideration that you're molding this human being for someone else before yourself.

I'm raising my boys to be sweet, kind, sensitive, genuine, caring, emotional, real, and respectful. Because men shouldn't be told they cannot cry. Men shouldn't be conditioned to be numb to their feelings like our world tells them.

I'm raising my boys to treat those around them with love and kindness.

To always prioritize their family.

To know the true value of love and to cherish it.

I will teach my boys to respect women.

I will teach my boys to empower women.

I will teach my boys to stand for equality.

I will teach my boys that they are not superior because of their gender.

I will teach my boys to use their strength for good and to do good and nothing else.

I will teach my boys to use the power that comes with carrying their gender for fairness. I will teach them to speak and radiate love.

Chapter 13

Stop Overprotecting Your Daughters and Start Over Educating Your Sons

We are so focused on preserving our daughters and raising the perfect little girls to become perfect young ladies that we easily lose sight of the immense amount of pressure we are putting on them.

We focus on teaching our girls the right etiquette while walking, talking, eating, working, and even playing. We focus on all that so they may be deemed "good enough" for the world we live in and the people we live alongside. We focus on teaching our girls that they cannot stay out too late because people will talk, simply because they are female, and females are fragile.

We fear for our girls rather
than believing in them.
We worry, rather than empower.

We need to teach our girls that they are capable.

We need to teach our girls that they are not 'less than' because of their gender.

We need to teach our girls that authenticity is much more important than conformity.

We need to teach our girls that if they fear judgement in every step they take, they will be living a life for others, an empty and meaningless life, an invaluable life.

We need to teach our girls that as long as their feet are rooted in honest goodness, the sky is their limit.

I want my daughter to know she is prized.

I want her to know she is valued.

I want her to know that she has so much potential.

She is so much more than pretty and sweet and cute and attractive.

She is so much more than the words that are used to define girls these days—they're all associated with their appearances and it's very shallow.

But she must know that she is intelligent and that she should be cherished and understood and treasured for who she is, no matter who she chooses to be. Not only valued for what she looks like, she must set her limits and standards where she sees fit for herself.

If there's one thing I can tell my daughter based on my experience of being a young girl, a teenager, a young lady, and now a mother, I would tell her to know her worth.

I would tell her to never allow anyone to sell her short. And to never, ever, sell herself short.

I would tell her that she can do whatever she wants as long as she's doing what's right.

I would remind her that she will know what's right if she's following the path that I've guided her towards. She will feel it in her gut, as we all do when we're doing something— right or wrong.

I'm determined to take all my life experiences and turn them into lessons for my daughter. I will take all the good and the bad out of what I've endured and make them stories by which my daughter can live and grow. I don't want her making the same mistakes I made because of the lack of support and lack of understanding I had growing up. I don't want her to feel forced into suppressing her goals and dreams and aspirations because of her gender or society or culture.

I will go against all odds to show my daughter that she can do anything, literally anything humanly possible regardless of her femininity. I don't want my daughter to ever worry about coming to me with her hopes and dreams and worrying that her gender will not allow her to achieve them.

I will not follow this pattern of brokenness and I will not feed it to my children, not to my daughter, nor to my sons who may have daughters of their own one day.

I will make sure my daughter knows that she is enough, always is, and always will be, no matter what everyone around her may say.

Chapter 14

It's a Cold World in which to Raise Children, Hang on Tight

I worry a lot and it's become rather crippling.

Since having children, I feel my heart has weakened and I've become soft. I worry about things that I know are not in my hands, but it does not stop me from worrying myself into a ceaseless spiral. It never ends well. I become obsessed and entangled in worst case scenarios.

The heart of a mom becomes
as strong as an unmoving mountain
and as delicate as the shell of an egg
the moment she becomes a mother.

I'm afraid someone will be the cause of a tear rolling down your cheeks.

I'm afraid you will be oppressed in any way, shape, or form, and won't be able to stand up for yourself because people can be unpleasant.

I'm afraid you won't feel worthy for some ridiculous reason when I know you deserve the world in itself; oh, how I wish I could give you the world you are so deserving of, my sweet child.

I'm afraid of what I may do if anyone tries to harm you, knowing I will stop at absolutely nothing.

I'm afraid of this world, my sweet children. I'm afraid it will engulf you.

I'm afraid this cold world will consume you and make you cold like its shell, but my dear children, you haven't even had the chance to see the pleasantness of its core.

I'm afraid you will see pain before you see happiness; life has a way of doing that.

But you must know my
precious children, that dark always
comes before dawn, but dawn
always comes, nonetheless.

I'm afraid you won't be able to count your blessings when you're in a tough situation.

I'm afraid to tell you the truth of it, that this world is half cold and shallow. Its people are partly dark and bitter.

Its days are long, but its years are so very short. Through its long days and short years, you'll have a million little stories of happiness and memories that will forever paint smiles on your beautiful faces, despite the cold and shallow.

But all this I won't tell you because, you see, I'm trying to sell you the world.

Trying to show you it will be wonderful despite our short years together.

Although deep down, I want nothing else but to hold your hands for eternity, to hold you tight where I can keep you safe.

Chapter 15

Don't Raise A Bully

Why can't everyone be kind?

I began asking myself this question when my eldest started school. I know getting used to a new environment can be a difficult transition for children and getting to know new people seeing new faces can be a lot to handle. I expected some sensitivity when he started school, but I never imagined my child getting sent to the office in junior kindergarten.

My son's first year of school was an overall good experience because it truly was a loving environment in terms of his teachers, but if I were to break it down and look at it one day at a time, my son struggled a great deal. I remember my young boy coming home one day after the next complaining about another boy in his class with whom he would have run-ins. Stealing each other's Legos, pushing on the playground, name-calling—you know that sort of thing that makes children believe their world has ended. I remember these days so clearly and I know the way my son would speak about this classmate; he spoke with such anger and frustration and, as a 4-year old, I don't know how he handled all these emotions.

But I understand now after all this time exactly how he handled it when I see his short temper and quickness to react to everything around him. He bottled it all in. I sent my child out into the world putting my full trust in an ill-equipped world and ill-equipped parents and a school system that focuses on applying Band-Aids* rather than dealing with the source of a conflict. And as a result, my son paid the price with all the rage I see in him now.

I do understand that kids have these feelings. It is normal to be happy, sad, angry, frustrated, we all experience this. But to have them consume a boy at just the age of four, that is a load too heavy for a child to carry. There is no justification for that.

It's hard for me to believe that we, as parents, don't play a vital role in this, if not the only role in this. It's hard for me to believe that if we stay on top of our children and instill kindness, that we won't have some sort of effect—some kind of positive effect.

Our children are imitators. They are watching us with great detail as if we were under the microscope for observation and replication, they're ready to mimic our every move, action, and reaction.

And we are the reason they behave the way they

do, at least to some extent. We are leading by example and whatever image they have of us is portrayed through their actions.

Our impatience can be seen through them.

Our kind-heartedness.

Our humanity.

Our attitudes.

Our outlooks.

The way we speak to them.

The way we speak about them.

The way we speak to others around them.

Most of the actions of our children stem from what they have seen through us.

We are the scale on which
they measure their failures
and their achievements.

It's all a ripple effect and if we pay close attention, we can see just how much influence we have on their every decision.

We must take advantage of having all this power at our fingertips and understand the responsibility we've been given. We have a responsibility to those around us and to the world in which we are raising our children.

Don't you think if we all implemented these ideas, we would be collectively raising better human beings? Maybe then we wouldn't worry about our children on the playgrounds and in the classrooms. We wouldn't worry that they may actually be capable of being the bullies themselves.

If we just commit to working on ourselves, we are taking a step in the right direction.

Chapter 16

Hold Your Children Through Their Tantrums

Today I comforted my son in the midst of a serious tantrum. People will often worry that if you provide comfort when children are upset or when they are lashing out, you're showing them that you're accepting their behaviour. I believe the contrary, and I only learned this through trial and error, like most of the things you learn while parenting.

> I believe that when I comfort my child through a tantrum, through the heavy emotions that he's feeling, I'm showing him that he is safe.

I'm showing him that these feelings are normal and validated and they don't need to come from an incident. They are feelings and we all feel, that's what makes us human. I'm showing him that together, we will work through these feelings and address them. We will not bury them and look away, allowing them to eat us up inside.

So, **I held my son today, while he pushed me away. He didn't want to show me his emotions. He was ashamed. So, I held him tighter and tighter.** Assuring him that I am here for him. Showing him that his feelings are accepted and validated. I held him so tight until I felt him wither away in my arms, I felt his shoulders release and his fists unclench. I could feel his heart releasing as tears streamed down his red burning cheeks.

I held him so close.

I cradled my not-so-little-anymore boy as he released all the anger that was consuming him. I was adamant about showing him that having these feelings was normal. This is okay. Feeling upset, feeling frustrated, feeling distressed, it's all normal. And I couldn't help but wonder, why shutting out emotions, especially for little boys was such a common and expected thing.

> **Why do we too often hear phrases like, 'boys don't cry.' 'Man up.' 'Come on now, wipe away those tears.'**

Why do we normalize burying emotions to little

kids that are just learning about having these big feelings?

We are conditioning them to be unemotional and compassionless. When a child is cold or hungry, we immediately attend to them without a doubt in our minds about the right thing to do. No questions asked; we know we must attend to them and keep them warm, fed, and safe. Yet when they need comforting, we try to label it as anything else but the need for love and affection, which is just as valid a need.

People will say, "They're just testing you." "They're just craving attention." "They're just spoiled." Whereas here are these little kids, yearning for emotional connection, which is embedded in our human nature.

We all need to feel loved.
To feel safe.
To feel protected.
To feel validated.
To feel human.
We all need to feel.

They are quite literally asking to be nurtured through their actions, yet we are so quick to label it as the opposite. Is it because the judgement weighs heavily on parents who don't discipline? Or is it to keep up with this culture of raising emotionless people who should merely coexist and not really live? Because if you're living without feeling, are you really living?

Why don't we try taking a different approach? Why not hold your child so close to your heart when he needs it most? Why not try to understand how deeply they're feeling disturbed and hurt and misunderstood regardless of their gender, regardless of their age, regardless of their mistake?

Why not discipline them through love, emotions, compassion, and patience, through all the things we see lacking in our world? They are the future and if we want to see a change, we need to *be* the change. It all begins with you and ends with you because when you send your children off into the world, they will continue what you started.

So, I held my son today.

I held him as tight as humanly possible.
Until I felt his anger drift away.
Until he felt the safety and love.
Until he was able to communicate.

I held my son and I told him it's ok
to feel. To be sensitive to those around
him and to radiate love and empathy.

There is no shame in a man crying. There is shame, however, in a man who knows no sentiment.

Chapter 17

Raising Your Children Means Raising Yourself First

Learning how to parent in the course of being parented is a struggle. Unlearning what you've been taught over the years and challenging your core beliefs is even harder, but very necessary. Core beliefs are what someone else thought was true and then instilled in you as you were growing up, but that doesn't make them right and that doesn't set them in stone.

> Questioning what you've been taught is natural when finding yourself and raising your children. It's a process of growth that is indispensable.

So, you were raised a certain way, and all was well, until you become a parent yourself. You go down the same parenting route using the same methods, because they feel familiar, until you realise that they're not good enough for you.

You see a flaw; you see contradicting ways. You do things that you really don't want to do, but you only do them because this is what you've been taught. You've been conditioned to believe this way was right and the process of unlearning is a difficult one; a road of self- discovery and self-training. A road of dedication to break a pattern that has been instilled in you, in order to change outcomes and to aspire for greatness. You may think to yourself, *well, I turned out fine*. And yes, you just may have. There is nothing wrong with that, but I always say in any situation that there is always room for improvement.

None of us are perfect
as perfection is
merely a perception—
it simply does not exist.

But can you do your best to get close? Can you try to adjust your ways in order to be more successful? Always.

Your child is the core of all the work that you do, and they need that cluster of support. The cluster is not what you've been taught, rather what you're learning about yourself along the way.

Our children are our best teachers since the day

they are handed to us once they enter this world. Growing before our eyes while we watch in such awe. Teaching us with every breath they take and every mistake they make. Through them, we will come to learn about a whole new world that was hidden from us. The world of becoming a mother.

Anchor yourself, as the seas are always changing, but you're as strong as the largest ship. You are strong enough to remain anchored and to show your children the way they should lean towards when the waters rock them. The path to kindness and righteousness. Because it will not be easy and fool proof, it will be testing and bittersweet. But with your support and guidance, your power is endless. Guide them towards goodwill and love and intelligence, but also be sure to guide them towards the creativity they show interest and potential in. You can guide your children towards the path you believe to be right and true while also believing in them. Believe in them, support their dreams, encourage their talents, empower them.

You will understand their motivation and their passion by watching them day after day as they bloom before your eyes.

It is crucial that you recognise that their dreams and hopes do not have to align with yours. If they're not challenging you, they're not growing and learning and figuring out who they are becoming, independent from you. They have a whole life ahead of them to explore, so don't limit them to the ways you've been raised. It was another life during another time. It no longer applies.

Chapter 18

Your Children's Childhood Doesn't Have to Mimic Your Own

For the most part, during my younger years, I remember a lot of happiness and laughter. There is no life that doesn't encounter a bumpy road here and there, and although I did go down a bumpier than usual one, I still remember so much of the good. That being said, there are also many experiences that have made me who I am today and have molded me to be the mother I am.

I am constantly trying to learn from the ways I have been raised. I try to take as much as I can from the good memories and I come to realise that now as an adult, those times were just as rough as the times I remember as a child, I was just too young and naive to catch on to them at that age. My most vivid memories, the ones that stuck with me, began when I was about 8 years old. I was old enough to understand when there was tension in our house. I would notice when my father wasn't around as often, spending his time with friends rather than his family. I would notice when my mother would try so hard to fill his shoes, she would carry the load and tell us lies to protect our young hearts.. I would notice when my father would try so hard to make it up to us when he was around, spoiling us with toys. From that time as a child, I automatically took in all the good and tried to bury everything else; that's what I find myself clinging on to today.

Remembering those times makes it a little easier on me when I'm having a rough day mothering and wondering just how much of a failure I was. It makes me think, maybe, just maybe, my kids will remember how they laughed with their siblings at the end of the night or how they had ice-cream before dinner or how they stayed up half an hour after their bedtime.

Maybe, just maybe, they won't remember that I was a mess that day, because I surely don't remember all the days my mother must have been struggling with us—somehow a child has an ability to take the pain out of the most difficult moments and turn it into the most memorable reminiscences.

I did have a tough childhood. I did have an even harder adolescent upbringing growing up in a broken home, but that only taught me how I do not want my children's childhoods to be for them. I will not shield my children from my storms, they will be there with me under the rain. But I will teach them how we must navigate the rough waters in order to come out dry; in order to be able to witness the sunshine once again.

Going through trying times as a mother doesn't make you 'less than'. It sure makes it harder for you to focus on mothering, and the guilt is doubled because you'll always feel like you're lacking, but you must be able to differentiate between struggling and being a "bad mom".

You cannot suppress all your problems and put all your efforts in shielding your children. You must understand that you are the most essential part of the equation here and without you, your children may not be able to thrive. It wouldn't make sense for you to put yourself on the back burner while focusing on taming the beast only because you're afraid—afraid of not being enough. Afraid of leaving a toxic relationship. Afraid of taking a risk.

You must be able to heal in order to be the best version of yourself for your children and shielding them isn't the solution. It's showing them that regardless of the storms, they are safe and loved. It's showing them that you will take the time to heal and put yourself first, for them so they learn to take care of themselves.

No matter how hard I try to shield my children and protect them from whatever may be happening in my personal life, it's not always the right decision. Children need to know that there will always be obstacles because no one ever walked through life without struggling. However, children must see you rationally deal with these problems. They must not see you tormenting yourself in the name of being a "good mom" and as a result, traumatise them because you were not in the best mental state.

Your hardship will affect them regardless of your constant efforts to shield them. Children are clever and they catch on to our feelings without us even saying a word.

Becoming a mother was difficult for me at the beginning because I wasn't sure what was right. I wasn't sure if I should be tough and strict and more of an authoritarian than an affectionate embodiment. I wasn't sure if being too nice might make my children too soft and not well raised nor well behaved and fit for society. I wasn't sure if I did things my own way, based on what felt right, I would be spoiling my children by following my heart and not my logic.

I wasn't sure of this because I kept comparing the way I was raising my children to the way I was raised. I look at myself and I say, *Well, I turned out fine*. And sure, we all say that until we realise, are we really fine?

This question always stops me in the course of parenting or making a decision that involves my children. I think back to my younger self, being a child in this situation and I always try to ask that little girl how she felt. What I would have given to be asked that as a child. To feel like my feelings mattered and were validated.

Our children have their own entities and are their own beings and we must be able to distinguish this if we want to raise them to be healthy young adults. We are all created differently and so unique—to assume we can all be raised and treated the same way would be very naïve.

I believe this applies to my good days during my childhood as well as my rough ones. Because surely there were many good days, I would be lying if I said it wasn't happy overall for me as a child. You just come to realise the truth behind certain situations as you grow older. There are many parenting methods my parents used I would never agree with as a mother, myself.

But I am not my parents.
I am not my mother nor am I, my father.
I do not have their experiences,
nor have I walked in their shoes
or lived through their struggles.

Their lives led them down roads that made them parent the way they did, whether it be good or bad. In their minds, they were doing the best of their abilities. They were giving it their all. In their minds, they were doing what needed to be done. It's hard to place blame when you condition yourself to give people the benefit of the doubt. That is a skill that is much needed if you're determined to heal and this is what I'm adamant on doing. I'm training myself to fully trust that hurt people, hurt people. Not because they mean to or want to, but because they are struggling that much.

I know my road today is different and that gives me so much power. I know I have resources and I'm willing to help myself and work on myself if I feel that I'm lacking or need guidance in parenting my children.

I cannot compare my
childhood journey to that of
my children's and expect it to fit.

Parenting is not one size fits all, but it is surely a lesson through time, and if you're just trying to repeat history, you're making a big mistake. Each day is a new opportunity, embrace the changing times and be welcome and accepting of change. Learn from your past and try turning your experiences into lessons you can improve yourself from.

Change is necessary for if you're not changing, you're not evolving and if you're not evolving, you're not learning and if you're not learning, I fear you're wasting your time.

Chapter 19

Your Parenting Methods Shouldn't Make You Uncomfortable

I had my first child when I was only 21 and I'd be lying if I said I had a clue as to what I was doing. Social media wasn't what it is today. There weren't multiple motherhood blogs and child wellness pages and sleep training pages and breastfeeding support pages. They weren't as easily accessible like they are today.

If you're on social media these days, there really isn't any excuse for you to be uneducated. Anything you need to know or have questions about can literally be found by clicking a button. But I remember when I was having my first child, it was very different.

I will admit I was very uneducated in the matter at the time, and I relied solely on the advice of my mother and those around me that were experienced, having been mothers themselves. I remember taking in so much advice from everyone and literally believing everything I was being told; barely questioning anything, if at all. I was fairly young and trusting and easily swayed.

I had some opinions as to how I would parent and

knew some things that just felt right that I would follow, but I admit that I was easily influenced. I wasn't confident in making decisions and sticking to them. I was very indecisive and insecure. But as my son grew older, so did my experiences with him and eventually, so did my courage. I began questioning what I'd been told and going down my own path; I began doing what felt right for myself. I had many regrets and I promised myself I would do better the next time around.

Today, three children later, I can finally say that I've begun seeing the way I actually want to parent. I have just learned what I really want for myself and my children and our futures— combined and individually. But it took me eight years of being a mother to finally be able to know—to really know—how I want to do things and with full confidence.

> I no longer allow those around me to affect my parenting or to shame me into doing things their way.

It still, until now, takes a lot of courage to stand up to people when they speak to and or about my children a certain way, that I may have been accepting of previously. Especially when the relationship is close, but it doesn't stand well with me anymore and

I've made it clear that it's now intolerable.

I no longer feel guilty if an aunt or an uncle or a grandparent says something that makes me stand up to them and possibly hurt their feelings. I no longer feel uncomfortable if someone at school says something to my child. I will go and address the situation directly.

> Being a parent leaves no room for being a pushover.

Leading by example also means I need to stick up for what matters to me, putting it first. And my family always comes first. My children are my priority and always will be and I will not hesitate any longer if that means ending a friendship or limiting family members. More often than not, setting limits is necessary.

There were many moments during my mothering journey when I found it was hard to be the parent I wanted to be around certain friends and family members and that didn't feel right. I learned that it was ok to put my foot down.

Relatives are a blessing and I've always loved big families, especially being raised in one. I have more cousins than I can count on my fingers and toes and I've always loved everything about it. Imagine having best friends that you could see all the time as a child and not just at school. It was and is honestly a priceless blessing. That being said, it also came with its challenges.

A tight-knit family like ours means not only your mother and father raised you. Your aunts, uncles and grandparents were always opinionated and tried to impose. They always had some type of effect on your upbringing.

Growing up, I lived this firsthand, and I believe it was an area in which my mother really struggled to assert herself. It was always hard for her to stand up to people who tried to interfere. She always tried to improve herself in raising us and was always open to the "help" as she saw it. Through my eyes though, being the child in the situation, it was aggravating and annoying.

That's what happens when there are too many cooks in the kitchen. A child easily gets lost in such circumstances and feels unheard. A child needs to feel the security from his mother and father primarily, and no matter how close the relation, any person that is not mom, dad, sister, and brother, is an outsider when it comes to making decisions. This is what my mother lacked to understand during our upbringing, and this is what I was determined to set straight in mothering my own children.

If you have all the aunts and uncles and grandparents raising your child, expecting your child to follow their leadership, then follow yours back and forth when you're so easily swayed, how will this child learn about security and real leadership? This child is now insecure and always seeking validation from others and completely indecisive.

I learned this early on in my motherhood journey after seeing it from a different perspective and it made me realise that **in order for my children to feel seen and safe in their homes and with their parents, they need to be heard and validated.** They need to know that any decisions their father and I take in their upbringing are ours and theirs alone and for their best interests, not for the validation of others. Our decisions are not based on what this person and that person might suggest. They need to know that even when someone makes these suggestions, they will remain that alone—suggestions. They will not determine the fate of any situation in terms of the upbringing of our children. It is now that it became clear that as much as I loved growing up in a large family, the older I got the more I realised how dysfunctional it was.

You'll learn this with time and through experiences of your own. It always starts with you and it's a series of choices you'll make throughout your life that will determine how your child will turn out. It will determine the relationship you have with your children. It will determine the friendships you will come to cherish and the bond that will be stronger than ever.

Don't allow the opinions of those around you to confuse you and your child and, as a result, ruin a relationship that should be treasured.

Chapter 20

Mom's Mental Health Matters

I remember the day I got into my car and just drove off to nowhere; open to going anywhere.

Anywhere but here.

Anywhere but home.

I just grabbed my keys and wanted any excuse to step out. I couldn't breathe. So, I walked out and drove off. Drove and drove down the long and open road, not wanting to look back. Not wanting to think about being needed by anyone and everyone. Not wanting to be asked for another snack, or a toy or dinner or to wipe a butt, or to wash hands or to put on socks. I didn't want to be called mom; I didn't want to be called babe. I just wanted to be me—unattached to any title that meant being needed by someone else.

I didn't want to be their everything.
At this moment I just wanted to be me.

Alone. Nowhere. No purpose. Nothing.

I just wanted to feel nothing. To do nothing.

I couldn't bear to feel this overwhelming exhaustion any longer. It was choking me so severely I was literally gasping for air; inhaling and exhaling just didn't do the trick anymore. I had forgotten how to actually breathe.

I drove off, trying desperately not to think twice about what I left behind.

I felt like I was breathing just
enough to survive but never enough
to really catch my breath.

Never enough to stabilize my heartbeat, never enough to quench my thirst for life. I felt like I was constantly walking on eggshells. It is extremely draining to be needed by someone for their survival and well-being; It's mentally daunting. A kid, a husband, a sibling, a parent, a friend. It's. So. Hard.

You easily lose sight of yourself because you are

not the priority right now. And by the end of the day, you are just re-winding yourself to do it all over again. But then, at the end of the day, you have your spouse who is expecting attention from you after a long day at work, and that's just the way it is because that's what you are; you're everyone's person.

You are the giver.

Of love.

Of attention.

Of safety.

Of survival.

Of comfort.

You are the safe haven to which they run.

You are the confidant.

You are the ultimate well that keeps on giving.

You cannot shrivel and dry up because they all depend on you for their survival and welfare.

You are here to carry them all through their burdens.

You're here to carry everyone but yourself.

Carrying everyone and everything takes a toll on you. Mentally tracking everyone's wants and needs and likes and dislikes is tiresome, to say the least.

Who tracks yours?

You just go with the flow because no one can do it as well as you.

You know the way your baby likes his pancakes.

You know what type of cereal your children eat.

You know how your husband drinks his coffee.

You know what can be thrown into the dryer and what will shrink.

You know when they have special events at school.

You know when they need checkups and new shoes and new toothbrushes.

You know everything, and without you, it just may all fall apart.

That's a lot of pressure—It's a huge burden for one person to carry. It's a load that weighs heavier than mountains. A mental load that is simply immeasurable.

So, with that, I drove off and I couldn't help but think to myself how much I didn't want this car ride to end.

Maybe I just wanted to keep going on this open road just long enough for me to catch my breath a little. Just so my heart would stop racing and my mind would stop pacing. Just enough for me to feel grounded.

So, I gave that to myself, because at that exact moment, I needed saving and I felt that I was way past that. And if I couldn't give that to myself, I would have burst. We are so much more than our messy moments, but it's much easier and much less painful to just dwell in them rather than attend to them, so we dwell. But I came to understand that allowing myself to make it to the brink of exhaustion and only giving myself a break when I'm that close to collapsing was not a solution.

Self-care is not self-care if you only take care of yourself when you cannot handle the pressure anymore.

That is just patching up a crack in the concrete with painters' tape; it will not hold. It's not healing the crack from the source in order for it to stop cracking. That is only maintenance and after maintaining something for so long, it will eventually break down and need replacing. I couldn't allow myself to reach that point again—the point where I felt like I didn't want to go back home—home where my heart always is, home where my absolute favorite people are, home, which should always be a sanctuary.

I would not allow this to happen again so I promised myself I would take these long drives as little gifts throughout the week. I will give myself the time to step away from the chaos for a little bit—just to re-center in peace so I don't forget how to breathe again. This motherhood gig is sticky, it's messy, it's a lot to handle. But it's also so much better than perfect because it's real. Exhausting yet exhilarating. And if you allow yourself that breath of fresh air every once in a while, whether it's a long drive with your favorite music playing so loud you cannot hear yourself think, or a walk you enjoy on a beautiful autumns' day, listening to the wind rustling the colorful leaves around you.

Give yourself these moments where you can remember who you are and what matters to you. These moments will save you from the dark nights of just wanting to get away to be nothing and no one. Because those nights, they can get very scary and very lonely.

Motherhood can be very dark at times, you just have to find your balance, so the dark days do not consume you.

Chapter 21

Motherhood is Misinterpreted

I truly believe being a mother is the hardest and the most misunderstood job. Unless you are a mother yourself, you may find this difficult to understand.

> Motherhood is the utter inconvenience of being the whole world for everyone around you— except yourself.

When I think of motherhood I think of supreme bittersweet bliss. So much love that it hurts, so much love that encompasses me, but also has me disoriented; I cannot seem to find myself. I find endless happiness in seeing my children smile and giggle, yet simultaneously find myself feeling inadequate, telling myself I can, and I should do better.

For some reason, this 'field' always has me putting myself down and setting myself up for disappointment. I'm constantly comparing myself to whatever new trends are happening on social media and whatever the latest celebrity suggested in helping get her kids ready without the hassle. I'm always looking to perfect the situation. I see myself merely as a cloud surrounding my kids, existing for them.

I will not be unfair, it's not all bad moments, in fact, there are so many amazing memories. There are so many little times that will just take your breath away. They'll leave you mesmerised and speechless. Tears of joy will fill your eyes more times than you can begin to count. The amazing moments are many.

I have so much time to myself. My husband is equally involved in raising them and keeping up with the house. But somehow, I still find myself agitated so easily, exhausted constantly, ill- tempered, and yelling too much. I can't explain it. I just don't have the will to do anything when I get the time.

The pressure put on mothers has been increasing at an alarming rate, keeping us on edge and on the brink of breaking. We are relentlessly worrying about how much we are doing and how we are doing it. About what extracurricular activities to enroll our children in and how to strategically fill their time in order to make 'good' human beings out of them; in order to make them great and useful additions to society.

Who's to say a child's calendar has to be so full they don't get a moment to breathe?

We have all forgotten how to exhale.

We are taking it all in from every aspect and jotting down suggestions and recommend-dations and listening to podcasts and reading the latest studies, that we are not grasping what it's doing to us in the process.

We have become so consumed by the idea of doing it all and following the latest trends for success that we have quite literally forgotten how to exhale. All we're doing is taking everything in without any let out.

We are setting ourselves up for failure due to stress and pressure and exhaustion and we are inevitably taking our children down with us.

We are leading by the wrong example. We are conditioning our children to believe that doing all the things possible, regardless of the toll it takes on our physical and mental health, is the right way to go. And it is the exact opposite.

I forget every idea I have if I don't write it down. My kids are either fighting, screaming, kicking each other, or spilling something; it's always something.

Motherhood is an eternal struggle between being a good enough mother and being yourself.

My identity is no longer mine alone— it now comes attached to this label of "mother" and is expected to be limited to just that. But it doesn't have to be that way. My motherhood journey does not and should not look like yours. It doesn't come in one-size-fits-all.

Comparison is the thief of joy and a trait we shouldn't be passing down to our children. What works for me can look the complete opposite of what works for you and that's perfectly fine and perfectly expected and normal. We don't want our children to be robots. The pressure we endure is enough on its own and we definitely do not need to be adding to it ourselves.

Motherhood doesn't have to be a competition. Motherhood needs to be all of us coming together encouraging one another. It doesn't have to be a life sentence in which you're struggling and suffering and miserable. It has so much beauty within it, you just need to learn to maneuver yourself. You shouldn't have to worry about what will happen to you if you aspire for more.

You should be able to ask for help in carrying a load that is truly not meant for one person to carry alone. A load that is so exhausting, it will leave you crumbled underneath its pressure like fine grains of sand.

Chapter 22

Motherhood is Your Rebirth

Your life did not end
when you became a mother,
on the contrary, you were reborn.
Your life did not end, Mama,
even though it sure feels
like that sometimes.

I know how lonely those first few months can be, and then the days following, and after that, and after that.

But this gift you've been given, it's a gift that cannot be appraised. A gift so valuable, that comes with such honor. Even though that in itself can put a load so heavily on you, it can seem rather unendurable. But don't forget yourself during those days. Don't forget you're still a person with a purpose. A person with wants and needs and a cup that needs to be filled in order to continue to give.

Your life did not end mama, even when it really feels that way.

It's easy to forget what you were before you became a mama.

What filled your days?

What did you do when you weren't breastfeeding and pumping?

What did you do with all the free time?

It's like time didn't exist before this. I know you feel like it's been put on hold for a while now, but that's ok. Think of it as a pause button on a movie you're watching. You'll get to it, I promise, just be patient.

Your life did not end mama. You can make or break this. Make the best out of it, or wilt and let it consume you, because it will in a heartbeat if you allow it.

Your life did not end mama. Some days you will feel defeated. Some days you will feel helpless. Some days you will feel fed up and those feelings are valid. But your life did not end mama, it's really only just begun. You are raising your child, making a difference in the world, forming the next generations to come. Shaping and molding someone to exactly how you see fit, giving so much love.

You have the most important job in the world. Your life did not end mama, it's only just begun. The days will go and come, you will watch sunrises and sunsets, and before you know it these weary days will be long gone; all you will be left with is the reminiscing.

You will get back to your purpose and you will have all the time in the world, but by then, believe me, your proudest moments will be the moments you were called mama. And you will have gained so much along the way. You will have poured out so much love and knowledge into your children and you will have set them on their ways to success and happiness.

Your life did not end mama, even though it feels that way. They'll tell you, "You'll wish these days would come back" while you are standing there with your hair in a mess, your eyes like those of a raccoon, wearing the same leggings for the third day in a row, because that's the most effort you can put in these days, thinking to yourself, *yeah right!* But let me tell you, in the midst of all of this, leggings, raccoon eyes, and all... my kids not even in their teens, but I do wish time would slow down for a bit.

That's only when they're not driving me crazy though. But still, your life did not end mama, even though it sure feels like that, just take a deep breath and don't let it consume you. **Remember it's just a pause button.** You will get your time and you will come out euphoric with a lighter heart and a breath of fresh air.

Chapter 23

All Along You've Been Guiding Me

Sometimes, it takes all my might to get up in the morning. My alarm clock will go off and I'll keep hitting snooze until I realise way too much time has passed and I panic.

Sometimes, I wonder how bad it would be if I just slept in and took the kids to school late, or if I just drove them to the drive thru for breakfast.

Sometimes, I wish I could just ignore the piles of laundry waiting to be folded.

Sometimes, I don't want to cook dinner.

Sometimes, I wish it was just me.

I miss being alone.

I miss myself.

I miss my own company.

I miss being my own person.

With all this longing, I tell myself it's only normal to not want to be immersed in this chaos. With its beauty, with its overwhelming love, with its rewarding feeling when your kids come to give you a kiss for no reason; even with all that, sometimes I don't want any of it.

Sometimes, the only thing I find myself looking forward to in the morning is a hot cup of coffee and I find myself dreading the chaos that takes place as soon as my children wake up.

Because sometimes my cup of coffee is the only thing I can enjoy after getting up at the crack of dawn and attending to these little adorable humans, wiping butts, making breakfasts they will refuse and packing lunches they will bring back untouched.

How little and simple of a reward, how insignificant it may seem, but how necessary for my well-being.

I've told myself this is my trophy.

I've told myself that I've earned it.

I've given myself something to look forward to when I don't want to get out of bed.

For that, I allow myself to feel accomplished. I allow myself to feel praiseworthy because I know I am, because I know this journey of motherhood that I'm on is not one that comes lightly and without regression, and somehow that's the beauty in it. It is rewarding beyond comprehension because saying out loud that "my son's smile makes it worth it" sounds fabricated, unless you've experienced it. Unless you've lived through the sleepless nights and the teething babies and the postpartum that knocks you off your feet and the body that you come to no longer recognise.

You must be able to cut yourself some slack. As insignificant as it may seem, you must grant yourself those little prizes.

I've learned to celebrate the highlights—as simple as my cup of coffee—because sometimes my sanity needs this cup of coffee when everything else is out of my control. I can feel all the blessings while also feeling exhaustion deep in my bones where no rest seems to extend.

Motherhood is not a clear sky
where stars shine bright.

Even though more often than not, after your longest day, you'll be able to identify at least one star, one small silver lining, one small inspirational moment in which you felt like you were winning. Regardless of how dark the sky may have been that night; you're going to reflect on how much you love that sky.

Within that sky lies your whole world, your whole purpose, whether the stars are present or not. Your lives will align and while all along you thought you were on this journey to teach and guide, to lead and nourish, somewhere on the road you'll realise that the paradigm shifted and all along you were growing, learning, blooming.

All along, through the long and tiring days, the innocent round eyes that are full of wonder and sparkle were there to guide you.

All along, I was learning about a whole new world, a more beautiful world, through you.

All along, you've been guiding me.

Chapter 24

An Empathetic Mother

To be honest with you, I didn't realise I was an empath until I started paying attention to my nervous system. Of course, this was only after I sensed my intense level of discomfort around certain people or in specific places and situations. I didn't think there was even a label for it, but we live in a world where everything must be labeled; you must be able to be "defined" by something.

So, here I am labeling myself.

Ever since I was a little girl, I've always cried during movies and that really grew with me. I fed it as I got older and into my motherhood journey in raising my own children.

Let me walk you through how it is to be an empathetic mother. Imagine your children's most intense feelings, add those to what you may be already feeling, now multiply that by how many children you have, and multiply again by 100. That's a lot of feelings for one person. What I learned about dealing with a young child's emotions is, more often than not, they're irrational and exaggerated. Learning to behave in these situations usually backfires on me. I feed off of their anger and frustration and I literally feel my head starting to throb almost instantly.

If they start to scream, I find myself screaming louder.

If they cry, I hold it in as much as I can, but you already know the bathroom floor is calling my name.

I'll be there falling apart.

For any parent, dealing with a child's heavy emotions is a struggle, but for the empathetic parent, it's multiplied tenfold. Sometimes, when I cannot deal with it anymore, I just give in to whatever they want. I know it's not the ideal solution, but if it buys me that peace and quiet for just a few moments, it's worth it.

Being an empathetic parent can be the most beautiful thing. It's not only the heavy and dark emotions that I take in. I also find myself inhaling their joy and breathing it out much more significantly—showering them in it. I just want to shout it out from the rooftops and show them how they have brought me such happiness. It fills me with a profound amount of love and bliss, making me feel as if I'm a balloon, weightless, carrying no pain, soaring up flawlessly.

It takes a lot of effort to contain my emotions

as an empathic parent, meltdowns are that much harder, and containing myself or trying to recover after the matter takes so much effort and dedication.

All of my feelings are heightened when dealing with my littles. These may be normal feelings for any parent, but if you're an empath like me, it feels so much heavier because it seems as if you're unable to rationalize.

It's taken a lot of effort for me to be able to disperse these emotions a little more evenly in hopes of toning them down, but I'm constantly trying.

Being an empathetic parent is trying, but it's not all bad. It can be a gift to truly help your child feel less alone when dealing with heavy emotions they themselves probably don't even understand. And I know it brings everyone joy when their happiness is multiplied and felt by those around them.

Chapter 25

A Mother's Mind Never Stops

This is how it went...

I woke up and promised my children some pancakes for breakfast. I started making the pancakes but remembered that I should quickly slip to the laundry room to run the dryer.

I found myself separating the whites from the colours while the pancakes were burning upstairs in the skillet. I ran upstairs because I smelled smoke. I quickly attended to the situation and continued to make the pancakes after clearing out the smoke. I finished making their breakfast and sat them down to feed them when I realised I hadn't been able to drink my coffee yet. I got up to make another cup because I refuse to drink coffee that's been reheated.

So, I set up the coffee pot again and it started dripping; making that beautiful sound that I love ever so much. I knew it would take a few minutes so I grabbed some chicken from the freezer that I should have thawed much earlier for tonight's dinner. That is when I realised I still hadn't run the dryer. I turned it on and said to myself, *okay, I'll just finish separating these colours in order to put in another load of laundry because we're low on socks.*

I finally finish the laundry until I'm summoned by my 3-year-old who had a milk accident— you know, the kind that makes you want to pull your hair out because your glass top dining table is a pain in the neck to slide off in order to clean the liquid that's stuck between it and the wooden table. Yes, that kind of accident. But it was just an accident, right? So, I began cleaning the milk and everything that had by then been covered in syrup.

What seemed like an eternity later, I'd given up on my coffee as it seemed like it's just not meant to be that day. By the time dinner time rolled around, I realized I had forgotten to take the chicken out of the freezer, so I resigned to order takeout.

Chapter 26

I Love You, But...

I love you with my whole existence,
but if I'm being completely honest,
I don't enjoy being stuck
in this moment with you.

If you're reading this and thinking to yourself that I'm a horrible mother for saying that, please, just give me the benefit of the doubt. Hear me out for a second, because if eight years ago I would have heard someone say that I probably would have thought the same thing. I wouldn't have known any better.

Eight years ago, when I got pregnant with my first child, I never would have imagined uttering the words

I love you, but I have no more patience for you.

I love you, but I just need to be away from you for a little while.

If you would have told me that I would be filled with rage eight years later, I would have brushed it off and called your bluff. I would have assumed you're just not doing motherhood right and there's no way that your feelings could be valid.

I never would have imagined myself sitting and watching my children in simultaneous admiration and agitation.

I never would have imagined myself thinking, what did I get myself into?

I never would have imagined wishing there was an escape.

But I guess that's what three children and eight years did to me. I guess that's what happens to you when you have to repeat every simple instruction 10,000 times a day. It's probably what happens when you're standing at the door for what seems like an eternity waiting for them to put on their shoes. Or when you're in the car begging them to stop fighting with one another because your head is going to explode. Or when you're praying the tantrum doesn't happen in the middle of the grocery store because the glares from strangers are going to make you loathe yourself yet again. Maybe that's what happens when motherhood just pushes you to the edge.

I'm hanging on for dear life,

but it feels as though I'm
slowly losing my grip.

It's an intense river of emotions that cannot seem to be contained, no matter how hard I try. It has me feeling as though I'm a volcano ready to erupt at any given moment every time I find myself repeating like a broken record. All of this only for my requests to be brushed off as if I were speaking to a wall, which at this point I'm sure would cooperate better than my children.

I feel the need to express my agitation, but I worry about how it will be welcomed. Would people recognise my pain and comfort me, or will I be judged for having the audacity to complain about something as beautiful as motherhood? Something that I must cherish, that so many can only pray to experience.

But then somewhere during the commotion, I'll catch a glimpse of my daughter's little dimples and become instantly mesmerised at this perfect human I've created. I find myself in awe and immersed in love.

But I also find myself torn between the immeasurable love and the crippling agitation.

I find myself wallowing in mom guilt and telling myself I'm not cut out for this—that I'm not good enough.

This is not the life I wanted nor the life my children wanted.

Who would want a mother that's constantly screaming at the top of her lungs to get her point across?

I wonder, how is it possible for me to love these little humans more than words can explain, yet instantly become so infuriated with them for screaming so loud and making my eardrums pop and my head throb?

Am I normal?

Does every mother feel this rage? Am I a bad mom?

Should I have never had kids? I'm riding this wave of self-doubt.

In the early stages of motherhood, it's all cuddles and marveling over this perfect child of yours. Regardless of the sleepless nights, it's as if you're on a love high. Drunken with attachment to this sweet being you've created, it's like you're in an eternal state of euphoria.

But the middle stage—the stage that welcomes the rage—that's where you get tipsy. **That's where you'll find yourself on the brink of breaking.** That's where you'll feel that time stands still. That's where you'll begin to question yourself based on these unwelcomed and foreign feelings you're having towards your littles. This is where I find myself struggling and drowning in self-doubt much too often.

"How hard can it be to tidy up your toys?"

"Why do you have to fight over this piece of Lego when there are 10 more of the same one?"

"Do you have to get that dirty when you eat?"

I ask myself questions only to find myself angrier; I'm constantly setting myself up for disappointment. And it's so, so easy to get sucked into the world of pity and wallowing. It's a dark hole that will keep taking whatever you're giving. It will pull you in and consume you.

I love my children, but my goodness they're driving me crazy.

This middle stage I'm stuck in, where they're not so little but not so big, it's tearing me apart. It's showing me a person I never thought I could be. It's showing me a part of myself that I cannot love, so how can my children love me?

It's showing me that I'm the mother I would have probably judged before I was a mother myself.

A mother that counts down until bedtime.

A mother that looks forward to school drop-offs and despises school pick-ups because that only means that the noise will be a trigger very shortly. This also means that the trigger will lead to a throbbing headache that will turn into a migraine that will make her feel like the worst mother ever.

This is an inevitable, draining, and consuming cycle in motherhood.

But it can't be like this forever, I tell myself. I know I can't be alone in this. I'm irritably struggling through trying to make it to the other side with some sanity left in me.

Although I'd be lying if I said I don't worry about the state in which I will finish; the state I will have put my children in during the long and painful process of becoming and being a mother.

Trying to pass the stage of missing shoes, mismatched socks, smeared food on countertops, and spilled milk.

These are the tiresome phases of motherhood—the ones we feel ashamed to talk about. But the real ones and the ones we actually should be normalizing.

It's not all fun and games and it's not all picture-perfect.

It's anger and frustration you never thought you would have towards your young.

It's rage towards little humans that you would give your heart and soul—no questions asked.

It's real and raw and painful and beautiful and all the things, all at the same time.

So, you must understand that it's normal to have these feelings.

It's normal to struggle in these stages.

It's normal to feel like you're lacking.

It's normal to doubt yourself.

What's not normal is questioning your love and ability to keep your children safe.

Because you're human.

Because no one is perfect

Because we all lack in certain areas, but that doesn't make us all bad.

.I know this because after all the rage I bottle up during the very long days with my children, when I put my head down at night, all I can think about are the little victories, the little moments where my eldest hugged his little sister to comfort her. The moments when they got along for split seconds while I was an utter mess searching for my phone to capture it because I knew it wouldn't last. The moment when my son told me this was the best day ever after watching his favourite movie together.

Even though I yelled, even though I was very impatient, even though through my eyes it may have been the worst day ever, these innocent children have a way of shining positivity on you when you need it most. They are so simple and so easy to please.

Just know that if you're a mother who is struggling with these difficult emotions, questioning yourself, and wondering if you were good enough today, these feelings and doubts should show that you are enough because you are trying. With every beat of your heart, I know you're trying. Please give yourself some grace.

Your worry only means you're doing the best you can and trying your hardest to be the best version of yourself for your children. It's hard, yes, but it's normal. Give yourself and others some grace.

Chapter 27

Marriage is Hard

Keeping track of this other person, while trying not to lose yourself along the way is difficult. At one point or another, as you grow together, you'll feel like you're just dwelling, you're merely coexisting, drifting along as the days swiftly pass you by.

And as the years pass, the memories will fade, the anniversaries will go and come, birthdays will pass; all while you're in the same loop, in this cul-de-sac of the life you're living. The most important occasions will seem purely mundane. It's not that you don't cherish them, it's not that you're losing love for your partner, but it becomes part of your routine.

And a routine can feel like a trap.

This relationship is hard to keep alive and well. To keep nourished and cherished. Good morning kisses will become underrated, *I love you* texts will be expected therefore unappreciated. Not because you mean to be unappreciative, but it becomes a habit and not something you do with passion anymore; it's just part of your to-do list now.

This relationship will be your greatest accomplishment and your greatest weakness. You'll be the most vulnerable you've been, yet strong enough to conquer the world.

You have already chosen to devote yourself completely and solely to your partner, but you never thought that some days you would wish that you could just be alone.

This relationship is defined by overwhelming love and joy; it's having your heart out of your control, out of reach. This relationship is being committed to giving it your all, all the time. You must do it all, he must do it all, there is no meeting halfway. As normal as you may feel it has become, as much as it has grown on you, as insignificant as you may feel the occasions are becoming, don't let these feelings devour you.

You must not stop putting in the effort.

This relationship is hard, but it's the most rewarding, it's the most satisfying, it's the most wonderful relationship one can have, if done right.

This relationship is hard, but when you've rested your head on your loved one's shoulder after a long day and felt all your worries drift away, that is priceless. Feeling the release, feeling the tension wither away. Simply feeling that another person carries a load with you.

That's what this relationship is about.
It's finding comfort and serenity when
and where you need it most.

It's knowing that there is no wrong or right way.

It's knowing that times will change you.

It's understanding and accepting that children will be a major turning point.

It's understanding your patience will be tested over and over and again.

It's understanding that you cannot possibly know someone like the back of your hand without going through thick and thin together.

This relationship is hard and to embark on such a journey and come out victorious, you must be willing to give unending grace.

Chapter 28

Our Love Looks Different Now

My dear husband, I loved you first and I loved you most, but it's so different now. At the beginning of our journey together, our life was long walks along the river, rain or shine. Now we think twice about muddy boots and umbrellas littering the entryway after these walks.

In the beginning, our life was date nights and movie nights.

In the beginning, our life was lounging around all day with not a worry in the world as long as we had each other.

Now we know all the words to the theme songs to Peppa Pig and Paw Patrol.

In the beginning, our life was driving anywhere and nowhere in particular.

In the beginning, our life was sitting on the creek's edge on that warm summer day, and fishing

until sunset with not a worry in the world. I don't think we have gone fishing again since then.

In the beginning, our life was long talks until sunrise, talking about what our futures may hold. We would imagine how many children we'd have, boys or girls. We would imagine how they'd sound and what it would be like to hear the words, 'mommy', and 'daddy'. Then we would fall asleep hand in hand, with my head resting on your chest; falling asleep to the way our heartbeats would sync in harmony.

In the beginning, it was only you and me.

In the beginning, you were the first and most important thing in my life. I couldn't see past you.

My dear husband, I loved you first and I loved you most, but it's all different now.

Today our love is not measured by long walks or deep talks.

Today, we're lucky we'll get a date night every once in a while, and by the end of the night, I'm usually exhausted.

I know that bothers you and I know you just want me to yourself, you just want to show me love and affection the way you do best, but our love is so much more than that.

I know you measure your success as a husband by how close you hold me and how well you love me in your own way, but our bond is so much more than that.

Our love is not defined by the minutes and hours together.

Our love is not defined by kisses and snuggles and

intimacy.

Though I cherish it all and need it, our love is so much more than that.

Our love is you being by my side even when I've given you the cold shoulder as a result of my exhaustion.

Our love is being hand in hand in raising our children.

Our love is understanding each other without the need to speak.

Our love is understanding.

Today, driving anywhere means strapping kids into car seats.

Today, fishing seems out of the question.

Today, it's not about you and me anymore because it's not just you and me anymore.

Today, we have little hands between us while we walk; little children sitting in our laps at dinner.

My dear husband, I loved you first and I loved you most, but it's so different now and that breaks my heart a little.

Today, you're not the most important thing in my life, you are my life.

Don't ever think you rank second.

Today, my being revolves solely around you and

our children; I simply cannot imagine a life without you in it.

Today, our long talks have shifted to what schools we will choose and what's on the dinner menu tomorrow.

Today, so much has changed and it's so easy to get caught up in the midst of it all, I just ask you to hang in there with me.

Today, our life is nothing like the way it once was, and it feels as though we get the last of each other. I hate making you feel that you get the last of me, but I promise you do not come in that order.

I long for our past. I long for a time when you were the only thing on my to-do list. I long for a time where I was never too tired to stay up late and talk. I long for a time where you didn't get the last of me and I didn't get the last of you. I long for us and what we used to be.

Today, we have what we once prayed for, and for that, I'm forever grateful. So, for now, if it means getting the last of each other, I ask for you to just hang in there a little longer with me. Take my hand and carry on by my side. Let us continue this journey hand in hand the way we started.

Know that my love remains as fierce as ever and only gets stronger. I've admired watching you grow into the father you are, and I'm so very proud to call you my mine.

My dear husband, I loved you first and I loved you

most, but it's all different now. Even though we seem to get the last of each other, I wouldn't have it any other way. I know you will be there holding my hand on the other side when our nest is empty, and our hearts are full.

Chapter 29

I See You, My Husband

I notice.

When you come home from work and run to our kids ready to play with them regardless of how tired you are.

I notice.

How you never leave the house without giving me a kiss, and never enter without greeting me with a kiss, adamant on making this routine meaningful.

I notice.

I see how you're trying so hard to teach our children through your actions. I see how you focus so much on showing our boys what it means to be a husband and father.

I notice.

When you don't share your worries with me to

spare me the pain. Even when you're spent and weary and need so desperately a listening ear and a shoulder on which to lean. I notice.

When you look at me and admire me even though I may look like a hot mess, which is most days since becoming a mother of three.

I notice.

When you give me the world simply through your love for me. When you make me feel like a queen, day and night. When you assure me always that everything will be ok, no matter the difficulty of the situation.

I notice your devotion to me and to our family.

I notice your sacrifice.

I notice your pure and selfless love.

I notice how your needs completely disappear when it comes to our family.

And I pray you know just how much I value your existence, for these words are merely a drop of water in an ocean of praises I can sing for you.

I notice all the small and all the big. I notice everything even if it seems I'm blank at times.

I see your efforts and I admire you for them.

Don't ever think you go unnoticed.

Chapter 30

Pandemic Parenting

As if parenting wasn't challenging enough, there I found myself parenting during a global pandemic. I'll be honest, I really didn't think this was going to be a *thing* and definitely not a *long-term thing.* Yet there we were, one year in and it was as real as it's ever was. To say my patience was, and still is, being tested on a daily basis is definitely an understatement.

When it started out, there was plenty of motivation involved because we all thought, *this will all be over before we know it.* I was not very worried about getting bored and depressed or mentally exhausted. Naturally, I decided to make the best of it.

Energy levels were high and rising.

I remember going to our local dollar store and stocking up on craft materials.

Amazon orders were coming in on a daily basis; our playroom looked more like a fun classroom now.

The crafts were never-ending.

Oh, and the baking. Let me tell you about the baking; I never enjoyed baking before, but here I was trying one recipe after the next, letting the kids bake with me and watching cookies rise in the oven.

The movie nights. The long walks.

The late nights.

My husband and I were on a mission to contain the situation in order to keep our children feeling safe and unaffected. I felt pretty successful in simultaneously keeping them busy and relaxed.

But surely not too long after, tempers became short-fused.

My patience was being tested.

My irritation drastically increased.

Confusion arose.

We no longer knew what to believe. I'm sure my children felt my struggle because they started acting out as well. They were so easily agitated.

They fought with each other for 90% of the day.

They refused to go to bed at night without putting up a fight.

They refused to eat anything I made anymore.

They had tantrums, full blown tantrums, arms flailing, feet stomping tantrums whenever they didn't get their way.

They no longer cared for their Ipad's nor the TV,

it was like I couldn't entertain them in any way.

My parenting strategy unconditionally shifted from 'making the best of a tough situation' to 'survival mode'. Without realising, all the pressure I was putting on myself to keep up with what everyone was doing, the pressure of 'the right way to parent during a pandemic' had caught up to me.

Spoiler alert: There is no right way.

At the time though, I couldn't discern that.

I couldn't put my finger on it then, but now I can see that it doesn't matter what that mom on social media was doing and how she was still baking with her kids 6 months into the pandemic. I would see posts like this and it would just put me down. **It would make me feel so inadequate and the guilt would consume me day after day.** It all came pouring down on me like a heavy waterfall—not the kind that is misty and leaves you refreshed; the kind that leaves you drenched and shivering.

I felt defeated and weak.

I was spent.

Spent from pushing myself to the limit.

Rather than focus on responsible parenting, I found myself feeling incompetent, which only lead to desperation and self-pity. I felt like I was lacking.

Caught between keeping up with what everyone on social media was suggesting—homeschooling, exercising, getting enough outdoor time, eating healthy, sticking to a bedtime routine, sticking to our "normal" lifestyles.

I even had myself convinced that I should be losing weight during this time and doing all these home workouts like everyone else on social media. But nothing about this was normal and I was clinging on so desperately to keeping up 'normalcy' in my home so that my children would remain unaffected.

The world was in crisis and we were in survival mode; confused as to what was right and what was wrong, and I should have just gone with the flow. I shouldn't have put all this pressure on myself to mimic what everyone else was doing during these difficult times. It took me a while to realise that what works for me doesn't work for everyone else and vice versa. It was time for me to stop comparing my mothering to whatever I was seeing on social media. This was definitely a time of clarification and revelation. I was trying to focus on responsible parenting so much that I didn't notice my children were struggling and I was the reason behind that.

I didn't notice how sad my children felt.

I brought this sadness upon them from all the pressure I was putting on them and myself. I was unintentionally choking my family under the impression that I was saving them from the craziness of the outside world. I forgot to recognize that they, too, were dealing with emotions much greater than their ability to grasp.

I should have faced those emotions with them. I should have told them the world is in chaos right now and that they had to just face the facts—we had to face this together. It was time to focus on what works for me and them instead of what was socially acceptable. They had to know that these feelings were ok. They had to know that life isn't always picture perfect.

> I came to the conclusion that, during a pandemic or not, there is no right or wrong way to parent.

Conformity feels very safe and stable, but it keeps us striving for external acceptance, which is a winding road that will keep luring you in, with no sight of an exit. It will suck you in and take all your happiness and peace of mind with it because it never ends.

My children were in shock and felt trapped.

I felt trapped.

My husband felt trapped.

We were all unintentionally affecting each other in negative ways. They too, needed to have some leeway while everything was a chaotic mess around them.

I desperately needed to rid myself of the idea that following social norms was the right way to go; there was nothing right about it. Our children are natural learners and are being taught by the world around them on a daily basis.

I needed to lead by the right example.

I was trying to make my kids
feel safe while I was falling apart
because of all the pressure.

If I wanted them to feel profound support, it was time I started ensuring their happiness is what truly mattered, whether it looks acceptable to the outside world or not. Whether or not we keep up with all the activities and the homeschooling schedules, if they felt safe at home even when the world was falling apart, and I considered that a win.

Chapter 31

Two Weeks into The Pandemic

It had been a couple of weeks, and the anxiety was beginning to kick in. The news and articles and warnings and precautions, they were becoming overwhelming. The weight of them had become quite unbearable and the thought of turning on the TV or radio or reading another article had me in a rut. It had become impossible not to panic. I unconsciously started to worry about my loved ones.

I'm worried about my kids, whom I fear I won't be able to protect.

I'm panicking that I'm not prepared enough—afraid because I don't even know how to be prepared. There are so many rules and guidelines now and I was just so confused.

Do I buy gloves?

Do I buy Lysol wipes?

Do I buy flour and canned foods?

Do I buy toilet paper?

What is going on with the toilet paper?

I found myself trying to prepare for the worst, yet

just thinking about that left me feeling sick to my stomach.

I wondered,

What if this lasts a long while?

What if I can't protect my family?

What if my husband can't work anymore and our business goes under?

What if one of us gets sick?

Oh my goodness the thought of one of us contracting this virus. My biggest fear was not being able to protect my family. My mind was spiraling over and over and over—around and around in endless circles of what-ifs and maybes.

What if my kids need medication and it's no longer available because people are going crazy and hoarding everything?

Will buying everything in sight keep us safe?

Do we need an escape plan if everything goes south?

Escape to where, though?

From what?

I didn't know what to think anymore.

I was sitting there trying to be rational, but the

media was just horrible. I'd been trying to stay calm but it was like a creeping ghost that was getting closer and closer to me, and it was only a matter of time before it breathed down my neck and sent chills down my spine. I'd try to rationalize, then I'd be hit with a "number of deaths so far" statistic. And before I knew it, I was all wound up and tense yet again, imagining worst case scenarios.

Society brought me to this state—people's actions.

The lack of humanity and kindness that spurred drastically.

That's what made me worry. I was more afraid of the way people began to unravel rather than the virus itself because, based on the facts, my family and I *should* survive if we catch it, based on our age and current health.

I was more afraid of humans than a virus that has taken over the world.

What a sad world we live in—a world where I fear for my children if a man's true nature is revealed.

A world where people jump on the opportunity to take advantage of humanity at its weakest point.

A world where it immediately becomes every man for himself.

A world, I fear, needed this exact situation to gain

some perspective, but it doesn't seem people have gained much more than greed and hostility.

I hung on tightly to my children and held them as close as I could. I could not have this take me down. I was a mess but I must be their saviour.

Do I show them that I'm afraid and that I'm nervous and confused?

Or do I carry on strong and insist on showing them that it will be alright?

I was very confused for a long time until I realized that if I kept shielding and protecting my children for as long as I was capable, how was I equipping them for a world that shows no mercy? What characteristics would I have instilled in them if they ever found themselves in a trying situation? They wouldn't know how to fend for themselves and I would be to blame.

So yes, **I did hold them close and protect them with all my might, but I did not hide the truth from them.** I showed them, to an extent that we were living in a dangerous state and caution was to be taken. I showed them what we were all collectively enduring.

I decided to teach them,
instead of shield them.

As the time kept passing, we had all established

that we were tired.
We're frustrated.
We're worn out.
We're anxious.
We're worried.
We're fed up.

But have we thought about how it's weighing down our children?

I was thinking about how I've been feeling lately as I watched my kids play on their bikes like they do all day, every day, limited to the perimeter of our driveway, and I noticed that they've been so easily flustered lately.

My middle child was usually the calmest of my children. He was always the sweetest little boy but lately, he's been yelling more than I'd like. As hard as I've been trying to shelter them and keep them busy, they were weary, and frustrated, and confused. It was inevitable and a part of me knew that, but I was trying so, so hard. I thought maybe to my surprise it just might work, but who was I kidding? They were feeling it all just like us. They were bored and tired just like us.

They don't truly understand why they can't play with the neighbours' kids or why they can't see their cousins. They don't really understand why the parks are closed. Time has stopped and the days are passing us by swiftly in bundles of madness while leaving our children disturbed, just like us.

To a young child, something scary is going on and they can't see the light at the end of the tunnel. Something simply beyond their comprehension. Something that has them feeling uneasy and with every right. Something causing disruptions and chaos in their small worlds. It's only normal that they've been affected by everything just like us.

When things finally started opening up in our city, I decided to take my kids to the park. Some of the parks were still closed off with caution tape, but some weren't and I had reached a point of indifference about the whole situation. So, I packed up my children in our car and we went. It was tremendously refreshing to see my kids having human connections outside of our group of family and friends.

Yes, I let them play with other kids.

Yes, I let them go on the swings and the monkey bars and touch everything there was to be touched.

They were so excited and played for hours. They were finally allowed to be kids again. It was like a breath of fresh air for them.

At one point, I noticed they just sat at the top of the jungle gym and talked with other kids, to which of course, I stood close by eavesdropping. The words that came out of my son's mouth shocked me. "Yeah, isn't it so sad how we just went to school one day and then we didn't go again and when we go back to school, we're going to be graduated? I'm not going to be in grade 1 anymore. Now I'll be in grade 2 and I didn't even get to say 'bye' to my friends. Isn't that so sad?" My 7-year-old was saying this to other children in close age proximity. And it hit me.

My kids have struggled
beyond my understanding.

They were so deeply affected by everything that happened, and deep down, I believe part of me knew that. So, I felt guilty for not addressing it earlier. I hadn't thought about the whole leaving school out of nowhere situation. He's never complained about it before, so, hearing him voice his concerns now was an eye-opener. Hearing these children take part in the conversation and seeing how they're equally struggling with these feelings of sadness and loss, frankly, broke my heart.

As parents, we try so hard to shield and protect our children and keep them from harm's way at any cost, sometimes overlooking the fact that

we can't always protect their little hearts.

We couldn't protect their little hearts from the loss that came with suddenly not seeing their friends anymore. My children were grieving the lives they once knew. We couldn't protect their little hearts from having these heavy feelings.

It's so easy to push our children aside and assume they're too young to understand and It's even easier to keep them in the dark.

We need to communicate better with our children.

We need to have hard conversations.

We need to understand that our children understand.

They are constantly watching and noticing and learning from us and everything around them. And just as we are humans, so are they. Just as we have feelings, so do they. Their feelings matter a great deal and we need to show them that.

We came home that day after the longest park visit we've ever had and had a long deep conversation about how their lives were flipped upside down.

We spoke about the friends they missed and the classrooms they won't see anymore. We talked about what would happen when they go back if they do, and what would happen if they don't go back until the next school year. We talked it all out and it was like a heavy brick lifted off of all of our chests.

> *I validated their feelings and showed them I understood. I spoke to them about grieving the loss of things and people and how a loss is a loss, regardless of its shape or form.*
>
> *I spoke to them like they were humans.*
>
> *I spoke to them that day with no barriers and I'm so grateful that I did.*

We must keep in mind that their feelings are valid and very much justified.

> We must keep in mind that
> although they may be little,
> they too have feelings bigger
> than they can comprehend.

I remember the time, recently during virtual learning when my son asked me, "Can we please just stay out here and play with our friends today? We haven't seen them in forever and we just want to play a little?"

He pleaded when I called out to him to come back inside because his lunch break was done. It was time for him to come back to a screen that he was attached to for 8 hours of the day.

These friends he was speaking about are our rear facing neighbors. They play together through our five ft tall wooden fence, merely sneaking glimpses here and there between the cracks.

I've watched them play hide and seek through that wooden fence. I've watched them bend rules of games in ways that the fence becomes part of their fun. I've seen them try so, so hard to make anything work, as long as they can communicate with each other. At this point it occurred to me, just how much my children missed socializing. They were desperate to just run around, throw snowballs in the air, make jokes and laugh out loud with children like themselves, free of worry and not tied down to rules and precautions and masks and hand sanitizer.

This is how much these kids missed being kids.

I won't lie and say I said yes to their request right away, because the guilt of having the teachers show up for my children while my children are playing outside just didn't sit right with me.

But as I sat there and watched them through the window, listening to their laughter and seeing the joy in their eyes, I didn't have the heart to take this moment away from them. I didn't have the heart to keep nagging for them to come inside and glue their eyes to the screen for another 4 hours.

And I understood their frustration. I understood their pain of missing friends and craving the slightest interaction, even if it was through a tall wooden fence. I recognised their desperation to have any human contact outside of our circle, and I would define myself as insensible to not allow it. So, I let them be, just as they'd asked because these kids were just asking to be kids. Playing and laughing with their friends whom they've missed so dearly, even if it's through a wooden fence.

Because a little happiness during a dark time is like a very much needed breath of fresh air.

Chapter 32

To Be a Mother

They ask me what it's like to be a mother
I tell them
I am vigorously agitated to become
Mother
I am coagulated to become
Mother
And whatever liquid is left of my being
Must solidify to become
Mother
I must be split into unlimited particles
To keep up with being
Mother
Fractions of my person scattered
Grains of my being become
Mother

And to maintain mother
I must continue to be stirred
Heaved
Boiled
Seethed
To be
Mother

I must be churned like butter
To become
Mother

And to stay mother
I will continue to give
To be
To stay
Selflessly
Mother

Acknowledgments

I want to start by thanking my husband, Mahmoud. This book wouldn't come to be, had it not been for you. You are my biggest supporter and always have been. You challenge me but remain a safe haven in which I seek solace. You've loved me through my messiest moments even when I know I was hard to love. You will always be home.

Thank you to my children, Jamal, Ali and Talia for giving my life purpose and meaning. You fill me with a love so deep I don't think I can every feel lonely, although that could either be a curse or a blessing. Thank you for being my inspiration for this book and for everything good I do in my life.

Thank you to my older sister, Zaynab. Though your love is mostly tough, it grounds me and always has me thinking 'I hate when she's right'. Thank you for always welcoming me with open arms when I disappear for weeks at a time, even though you hate it when I do that.

Thank you to my younger siblings, Nour, Zosta and Moe for your continuous and unparalleled love and support. We have a powerful bond and I cherish you all more than you'll know. You all have hearts of gold. Thank you for believing in me.

Thank you, mom, for doing the best you can in raising us during the hardships you endured and through the silent struggles that you battled; your sacrifices do not go unnoticed. Thank you for being a wonderful grandmother to my children and encircling them with loads of love. No amount of thanking you will suffice. I love you.

Thank you, Sara, the sister I chose. Thank you for encouraging me to do better in every step I take. Thank you for being so genuine and providing me with a safe space where I can always speak my mind freely without a single doubt that a word will be taken out of context.

Thank you Diala, for being my voice of reason. For allowing me to always feel secure knowing I can count on you, no matter what. Thank you, mostly, for being the epitome of a true friend.

Thank you to all my cousins whom I love so dearly. Joujou, Loulou, Zeinab, Fatme, Abbas, Jihad and Zari. You guys fill my heart with happiness, and because of you, the walls of my house are saturated with the most beautiful memories. You all supported me every step of the way and lifted me when I felt like I was lacking.

Thank you to my friends, Nadine, Nariman, Hiba and Sara. You ladies are the definition of women empowerment. I came to you all countless times and asked for your guidance and support and as always, you assisted me. Thank you for being genuine friends, I cherish our bond that only gets stronger as the years go by.

Thank you, Moose for your extensive support that literally saved me. You are selfless and always willing to lend a helping hand and for that, my words will not portray the amount of gratitude I feel for your kindness. Thank you for sharing your impressive knowledge with me and for your boundless generosity. I wish I can return the favor one day.

Thank you Leslie Means for creating such a beautiful space on the internet that is so welcoming and safe. You and your team at Her View From Home were the first people to believe that my words held meaning and deserved to be shared, you gave me the push I craved to make it to where I am today.

Thank you to Brynn and Heidi, my editor, and my designer. Your help did not end at answering questions about editing and designing. You reassured me when I felt lacking and went above and beyond to show me how much you liked my words by answering my endless questions and keeping up with my emails that went back and forth. You helped me figure out what I wanted, even when I didn't know what that was. I have enjoyed working with you both greatly, and I cannot wait to do it again.

Thank you Tumkeen, for your guidance throughout this painstakingly exciting process. You were my go-to person and always kept me on top of my game. Thank you for being in my corner, I wish I can reciprocate for you one day.

Thank you to my amazing launch team, each one of you have been so helpful and kind and I appreciate you all tremendously. Thank you to every reader that has supported me along the way, near and far. Whether you're a supporter on social media or a friend or simply an acquaintance. You've all played a vital role in my success and motivated me. Thank you for following along and reading my words. I wouldn't be here without all your support.

www.ingramcontent.com/pod-product-compliance
Lightning Source LLC
LaVergne TN
LVHW050959080826
845145LV00009B/2371

* 9 7 8 0 5 7 8 9 2 7 2 1 3 *